HOW TO
ORGANIZE
YOURSELF

CREATING SUCCESS

The best-selling series is back and better than ever

MARCH 2013

Because you only have one chance in life to make a good impression.

HOW TO ORGANIZE YOURSELF

JOHN CAUNT

CREATING SUCCESS

KoganPage

Publisher's note

Every possible effort has been made to ensure that the information contained in this book is accurate at the time of going to press, and the publishers and author cannot accept respon~~sibility for any errors or omissions, however caused. No re~~sponsibility for loss ~~or damage occasioned to any person acting, or refraining from~~ action, as a result of ~~the material in this publication can be accepted by the editor, or~~ the publisher or the ~~author.~~

First published in 2000 ~~by Kogan Page Limited as *Organize Yourself*~~
Second edition 2006
Third edition 2010
Fourth edition publishe~~d in 2013~~

Apart from any fair dea~~ling for the purposes of research or private study, or critic~~ism or review, as permitted un~~der the Copyright, Designs and Patents Act 1988, this publi~~cation may only be reproduce~~d, stored or transmitted, in any form or by any means, wi~~th the prior permission in wri~~ting of the publishers, or in the case of reprographic repro~~duction in accordance with the ~~terms and licences issued by the CLA. Enquiries concerni~~ng reproduction outside these terms should be sent to the publishers at the undermentioned addresses:

120 Pentonville Road   1518 Walnut Street, Suite 1100   4737/23 Ansari Road
London N1 9JN   Philadelphia PA 19102   Daryaganj
United Kingdom   USA   New Delhi 110002
www.koganpage.com   India

© John Caunt, 2000, 2006, 2010, 2013

The right of John Caunt to be identified as the author of this work has been asserted by him in accordance with the Copyright, Designs and Patents Act 1988.

ISBN   978 0 7494 6718 0
E-ISBN   978 0 7494 6719 7

British Library Cataloguing in Publication Data

A CIP record for this book is available from the British Library.

Library of Congress Cataloging-in-Publication Data

Caunt, John.
How to organize yourself / John Caunt. – Fourth edition.
  pages cm
  ISBN 978-0-7494-6718-0 – ISBN 978-0-7494-6719-7 (ebk.)   1. Time management.
2. Personal information management.   3. Life skills.   I. Title.
  HD69.T54C39 2013
  650.1'1–dc23   2012045504

Typeset by Graphicraft Limited, Hong Kong
Printed and bound by Ashford Colour Press Ltd, Gosport, Hampshire

CONTENTS

INTRODUCTION

Never have we experienced a greater need to be organized.

The working environment of today is characterized by constantly rising pressure to deliver with fewer resources. Against a background of restructuring and cost-cutting we are expected to keep a larger number of balls in the air and to do so with less support. The picture is increasingly one of self-sufficient professionals responsible for all aspects of their workplace organization. The information age provides us with some of the tools to organize our working lives, but it also presents us with many new challenges in the form of increased volumes of information, constant connectedness, expectations of immediacy, and interruptions to our routines.

Outside our working lives, we have greater expectations of our leisure time, and we readily expect to be able to fulfil family commitments while we and our partners hold down demanding jobs. We juggle the different elements of our lives to cram in trips and excursions, duty visits, entertainment, house-keeping, health pursuits, personal development, voluntary responsibilities, family activities and time with friends.

To cope with all of this we need to be organized. We need to handle time, information, people and technology as efficiently and effectively as possible in order to deliver the results on which we will be judged. Being organized means:

- less time spent firefighting and responding to crises;
- sharper focus on the things that matter most in terms of producing results;

- the ability to see your way through complex problems and challenges;
- more time for family, friends and leisure;
- reduced stress and fatigue;
- greater sense of achievement;
- the chance to step back and take pride in a job well done.

Even though the benefits of greater organization are clear, we present ourselves with excuses for failing to acquire them:

> **Excuse 1** – *'The ability to be organized is something innate. It's a quality that you either possess or lack, and I just don't have it.'*

Certainly it's true that we vary in our natural tendency towards being organized, but it isn't true that there is nothing we can do to overcome that inclination. Studies of brain function have revealed differences in the way that the two hemispheres of the brain operate. Work by American psychologist Jerre Levy and others demonstrated that the left hemisphere is superior in analytical functioning, while the right hemisphere is superior in many forms of visual and spatial performance and tends to be more holistic in its functioning than the left. It has been shown that although we use both hemispheres of the brain simultaneously, there is a tendency in most of us to favour one side or the other. We are either left-brain dominant or right-brain dominant. In simple terms, the left-brain dominant person tends towards an organized, analytical and methodical approach, while right-brain dominant types tend to be more creative and intuitive. However, just because we may favour one way of operating, it does not mean that we are unable to develop the skills associated with the other hemisphere. In truth, we all display skills associated with both sides of the brain and our overall thinking and learning benefits from efforts to strengthen those elements that don't come so naturally to us. When it comes to organizing skills, the right-brain dominant person may just have to work a bit harder at it than the left-brain dominant individual. And just in case you are wondering, I'll own up now to being a person who has to work quite hard at being organized.

Excuse 2 – 'There is no way that I could be organized in this place. The constant interruptions, the crises, the disorganized colleagues.'

Yes, there are plenty of workplaces where it is hard to be organized, but that is no reason to give up. In the chapters that follow we will look at how you can take control of your working environment and reduce interruptions and distractions. We will look at the effect of good planning in forestalling crises, effective delegation which minimizes colleague dependency, and ways of helping others to be more organized.

Excuse 3 – 'I would like to be more organized but I'm just too busy to spend time on it at the moment. Perhaps in a couple of months' time.'

In today's work climate, the person who postpones action in the hope of having more time a month, two months, six months from now, is destined to be forever disappointed. And what does 'being too busy' really mean? It is possible to spend your working days scurrying in every direction and achieving little – you may be busy but not effective. Targeted activity is what brings results, and improved organization is largely about targeting your activity.

For many of us the aim of getting organized has a great deal in common with those other ubiquitous lifestyle objectives – getting fit or losing weight. We believe it will be good for us and our lives will be fuller and more satisfying if we can accomplish it, but somehow we never seem to achieve it to the degree or with the consistency we seek. In the same way as we embark on successive diets and fitness programmes, so we pitch ourselves into organizational splurges that may bear fruit for a while before we sink back into our depressingly chaotic old ways. We latch onto some new regime or rush to acquire the piece of equipment or software that we believe will solve our organizational problems for us. And perhaps, for a time, it seems to do the trick. But then we lose our focus, the old habits start to reappear, systems go down the tubes and procrastination is the order of the day.

It doesn't have to be like that. Everyone can become more organized – and not just for a month or three months, but permanently. However, there's no instant fix – sustainable change requires more than a new gadget or a few quick tips. It requires attention to your current attitudes and expectations, a degree of perseverance in building new routines, and readiness to pull together all the threads – time, information, people and technology – to produce a package of actions that will work for you.

So, if you have made previous attempts at better organization that haven't worked out, don't despair. You can do it, and I hope this book will provide you with many of the strategies needed to get you there. But don't adopt everything I suggest religiously: be prepared to adapt or experiment with what is written here and build a system that is not mine, but yours.

Whilst most of the examples used in this book are work related, the principles and strategies suggested are just as applicable to those seeking to bring better organization into their home, leisure or voluntary activity. Nor, from a work point of view, should it be assumed that there is any perceived target audience in terms of occupational groups or levels of workforce seniority. The pressures of the modern workplace are fairly universal, and the steps to improved personal organization are pretty much the same whatever your job. There will be differences, of course, in the volumes and nature of information you are required to handle, the amount of support you are able to call upon and the number of colleagues, clients and contacts you have to relate to. But whether you are a newly appointed junior, an established professional or a self-employed home worker, there is something here for you.

In those sections that deal with aspects of technology, it is assumed that most readers will have some awareness of computers but that their knowledge may be piecemeal. The speed of technological advance and the proliferation of electronic devices and applications mean that detailed and up-to-date coverage of available options is impossible in a short book such as this. However, I have used as examples some of the most popular or well-regarded applications at the time of writing.

KNOW WHERE YOU ARE GOING

This book contains information on a whole range of techniques, technology and tips to assist with your personal organization, but none will do the trick without the first essential ingredient. That is you and your approach to the process of becoming more organized. The first step to being organized occurs not in your inbox, your filing cabinet or your computer, but in your head. If you are to take control of your life and begin to make a difference, you must address your organizational weaknesses and strengths, the reasons for current disorganization and your attitude towards changing the situation. You should ensure too that you have a clear idea of where you are heading and how you expect to get there.

We all have our organizational strengths and weaknesses, so before going any further take a moment to ask yourself where your particular shortcomings lie. Which of the following statements apply to you?

- There is a lack of overall direction to my work.
- I have difficulty extracting priorities from the mass of tasks and issues that come my way.
- My days seem to slip away with little achieved.
- I don't plan my time adequately.
- I end the day with more items on my 'to do' list than I started with.
- I find it hard to estimate how long some tasks are going to take.
- Deadlines seem to creep up on me.
- I'm not sure that I make best use of the times when my energy levels are highest.
- I flit in and out of routine tasks, often letting them interrupt more important work.
- I tend to postpone tasks I don't like.
- Trivial tasks assume greater importance than they should.
- I sometimes have difficulty knowing where to start on complex tasks and projects.
- I would like to be more systematic in my decision making.
- The volume of incoming correspondence is a problem for me.
- I don't often tackle messages and documents when I first look at them.
- I am often unable to decide what to do with information I receive.
- I would like to assimilate documents more quickly.
- I forget a lot of what I read.
- I find myself attending too many unproductive meetings.
- I don't think I delegate enough.
- Colleagues bombard me with information I don't need.
- I am plagued by interruptions.
- Too often I take on tasks I should refuse.

- My workspace layout isn't conducive to good organization.
- There are piles of paper in my office, my desktop is cluttered and cupboards and drawers are crammed.
- I spend a lot of time looking for things.
- My files are disorganized.
- I am concerned that I am not adequately utilizing technology to organize my work.
- I don't use the internet as effectively as I might.
- My personal organization declines when I am working from home or away from the office.

REASONS FOR DISORGANIZATION

The above checklist aims to help you identify some of your current organizational weaknesses, but it's useful also to explore the reasons for them. In broad terms we could say there are three main drivers of disorganization: external pressures, systems failures and personal factors. The first includes such things as overload, interruptions, and problems with the working environment, while the second relates to absence of strategies and routines for managing time and information, and failure to use tools appropriately. It is the third area that we most often neglect. Personal factors affecting disorganization might include anxiety about certain tasks or a desire for novelty that leads us to flit from one task to another. Also present might be a tendency towards perfectionism, a habit of taking on too much, an unwillingness to delegate or a failure to say no on occasions. All of these problems can be tackled, but first they need to be recognized, so take a moment now to ask yourself this question: 'What are the main reasons why I am currently less organized than I would wish to be?' Jot down your responses. They will be useful in an objective-setting activity later in the chapter.

ATTITUDES TOWARDS ORGANIZING

Disorganization is not, in the main, something about which we feel a sense of shame. In fact we can present it to ourselves as almost an endearing quality – an indication that there is more to us than boring routines, rigid attention to maintaining schedules or an obsessive desire to ensure that everything is in its proper place. As long as we persist in such attitudes, we are likely to hold some inner resistance to becoming more organized, and the changes we seek will be more difficult.

In the Introduction I presented some of the excuses we give ourselves for not becoming more organized, but sometimes there are more than just excuses. We may have entrenched beliefs about ourselves that hold us back even when we have decided to act. Beliefs such as these can lead us to doubt our ability to change:

- 'I've been like this so long I'm not sure I can change my ways.'

- 'I'm just naturally untidy.'

- 'I'm so easily distracted – can't keep my attention on anything for long.'

One way to shift such unhelpful beliefs is to search out contrary evidence. Take a good look at your life and the likelihood is you will be able to find areas where you are organized. Perhaps good organization is apparent in some leisure interest to which you are able to give time and attention despite your otherwise busy schedule. Maybe it occurs in aspects of your domestic arrangements. Even in areas of your life where chaos appears to rule, there will be pockets of good organization – items that are stored where you are always able to put your hands on them and routines that get the job done quickly and effectively. What is it about these aspects of your work or your life that has made them different? Are there features of your organizational successes that you can transfer into other elements of your life? Focus on the things that are working well in addition to those that are not, and use them to build a more positive view of the way forward. Have a go now at listing your organizational strengths – the things that are working well for you, in whatever area of your life they are to be found. Writing them down will generally add to the value of the exercise.

If you are to remove unhelpful attitudes towards organization, it is also important to weed out any negative self-talk. Statements like 'I'm never able to muscle down to tasks', whether made privately to yourself or shared in conversation with others, only serve to reinforce a sense of helplessness. Replace them with positive affirmations – simple strong statements repeated regularly to yourself: 'I can achieve everything I set out to do.' 'I can handle interruptions and get back on track.' 'I can change disorganized habits.' 'I can cope with whatever the day throws at me.' Choose some affirmations that are right for you and mentally repeat these statements of faith in yourself on a regular basis.

It's essential too that you shift any attitudes that may reinforce the notion that organization is a wholly tedious process or that disorganized people are somehow more interesting than their more organized colleagues. Visualize the benefits of a better-organized life style. How will it feel? What will better organization offer you that you don't have at present?

Visualizing the benefits of greater organization is made easier if you have a clear view of what your objectives actually are, but in a busy, multifaceted life this may be more easily said than done. You may have a host of vaguely articulated goals, commitments and aspirations. Some will overlap; some may conflict. There will be those that you have originated and others over which you have little control. They may be associated with any of the elements that constitute your life: work, leisure activities, family and relationships, voluntary responsibilities, learning and development.

At a later stage in the process of becoming more organized it may be useful for you to spend some time shaping up a coherent set of life objectives, but for now let me ask a simple question that, in the context of this book, helps to identify some of the things that are important to you.

WHY DO YOU WANT TO BE MORE ORGANIZED?

Ask yourself that question now. Jot down all the answers that come to mind and follow any trail that an answer generates.

Example

Q. Why do I want to be more organized?
A. So that I don't have to work so many hours.

Q. How would I wish to use the time saved through greater organization?
A. Getting fit; learning Spanish; spending more time with the people I care about.

Q. Why do I want to get fit?
A. Ability to take part in a range of outdoor activity, greater confidence and self-respect.

Q. Why do I want to be more organized?
A. To show that I'm on top of my job.

Q. Why do I want to show that I'm on top of my job?
A. To demonstrate that I'm worthy of promotion.

Q. Why do I want to be more organized?
A. To gain a greater sense of satisfaction from the projects I undertake.

Q. Why am I seeking that greater sense of satisfaction?
A. Because all my activities currently feel like chaotic drudgery. It doesn't have to be like that.

Pursuing this question helps to shift the sort of negative attitudes I was referring to earlier and reinforces the point that the changes you are seeking are not ends in themselves, but means to achieving those things that are really important in your work and your life in general.

An understanding of broad aims is an important starting point to becoming more organized. But the next essential step is to identify the practical things that will have to be accomplished if you are to achieve those aims, and that means giving some attention to setting objectives. Let's take a look at objective setting now.

SETTING OBJECTIVES

Whether you are thinking about major life goals, the requirements of a work project or the process of becoming more organized, time spent determining your objectives is more than likely to be repaid. Unfortunately, objective setting is often hedged around with a certain amount of jargon and mystique that can deter the uninitiated. But it doesn't have to be a big deal. An objective is just a tool, the purpose of which is to transform amorphous challenges into tasks you can get your teeth into and that will lead to meaningful outcomes. It needs to be clear and precise, but don't go overboard in your search for complete precision. An objective that is a little loose is better than no objective at all. This is particularly the case when you are setting objectives for yourself rather than for others. You know what you mean; others might not.

Try to produce objectives that are SMART – specific, measurable, achievable, results oriented and time related.

Specific

The more general an objective, the harder it is to focus on those tasks and activities necessary to bring about its achievement. As an example let's consider your purpose in reading this book. You're doing it because you want to become more organized. That's OK as a general aim but it's not much help in getting to where you want to be. For that, you need to break your general aim down into objectives that are more specific in terms of the things you are going to do. The specifics are those things you may already have identified as weaknesses to be resolved – for example, overcoming procrastination, clarifying priorities or eliminating clutter.

Measurable

Without a measurable element to your objectives you have no way of determining at what point they have been achieved, and the resultant vagueness may mean a loss of focus. You might decide, for example, that one of your objectives in respect of personal organization is to improve your typing speed. But what constitutes successful achievement – an improvement of one word per minute, or an improvement of 30? Only with some idea of scale does the objective have precision. And don't neglect the fact that there may need to be more than one measurable element if an objective is to have any value. An increase in typing speed of 30 words a minute may be entirely achievable but at a cost to accuracy that renders the improvement meaningless. Whilst you may be prepared to sacrifice some degree of accuracy in the initial drive towards increasing performance, you will want to ensure that such losses are recovered later on. However, don't be too rigid or arbitrary in the measurable elements you introduce to your objectives. Excessive quantification may actually hamper achievement as attention spent on measuring gets in the way of what is being measured. And lack of flexibility may mean that you hit a brick wall when unforeseen obstacles appear, or may even lead you to ignore opportunities for further development beyond the stated target.

Achievable

Any objective you set should be achievable. The reason you are using the objective is in order to get things done and to obtain the positive reinforcement that comes from success. It is not the purpose of objectives to add unnecessary stress to your life and deliver the negative reinforcement of failure. On the other hand, there is little to be gained by setting objectives that can be achieved with minimal effort. You may get a slight buzz when you cross them off your list of things to do, but deep down you won't be fooled by the illusion of progress. The trick is to set immediate objectives that are just out of reach. It's a matter of having to stretch yourself to achieve them, but not to saddle yourself with aspirations that will be impossible to meet.

Does that mean that you can't have a grand objective – a target that is well beyond your current capabilities? No, it doesn't, provided that you break down your main objectives into sub-goals and work towards your grand vision in manageable steps.

You might, for example, have a grand objective of reducing the weekly hours you spend on work matters from a current average of 55 to an average of 40, while maintaining current levels of output and quality. This is most probably a target that will require attention to many of the elements covered in this book, and should be broken down into sub-goals, each with realistic stages towards achievement. One such sub-goal might concern improved ability to delegate. But within this there needs to be recognition that the early stages of such a process might actually mean an investment of more time, as you give attention to such activities as identifying those tasks it is possible to delegate, briefing the people who will take them on and working to ensure that the tasks are perceived as valuable and challenging. Your staged objectives should take account of this time investment and provide the space for it before the time savings start to kick in.

Results oriented

Objectives should be described in terms of results delivered rather than activities. If, as part of a drive to become more organized, you determine that you will arrive at work an hour earlier in the mornings, this simply describes the activity. You can spend that hour drinking coffee and chatting, and you will still meet the objective. A far better objective would include identification of those things you propose to achieve in the hour – possibly the completion of tasks that require uninterrupted concentration and are therefore more difficult to accomplish in the hurly-burly of the regular working day.

Time related

Objectives generally benefit from clear deadlines by which they will be completed. This links closely with the requirement that they be achievable. An objective may be achievable in one time-scale but not in another. Deadlines are also helpful in providing motivation and maintaining momentum, provided that they are related to a period of time that you are able to get hold of. A deadline six months hence is too vague and distant for most of us. If we are to maintain consistent effort and motivation for a period of more than a month, then we will generally benefit from breaking our target down into smaller stages – individual weeks or months. This may mean building in monthly milestones – review points on the road to your main goal – or setting a series of sub-goals. If, for example, you conclude that it should be possible over a period of three months to reduce the amount of time you spend in meetings from a current average of 12 hours a week to 6, you might set staged targets of a two hour per week reduction in each month with a specific monthly focus:

- Month 1 – extricate yourself from unnecessary meetings.
- Month 2 – find more time-efficient alternative ways of doing some of the business currently conducted in meetings.
- Month 3 – improve the efficiency of those meetings you remain involved with.

Activity

What are your objectives in terms of better organization? You gave some thought earlier in the chapter to why you want to be more organized, but it's time to get more specific. In the light of your responses to the checklist of current weaknesses, your analysis of the reasons why you are not as well organized as you might be and your answers to the question 'Why do you want to be more organized?', have a go now at articulating your main goals in respect of better organization. Write them down, taking account of the above SMART points. In some cases, you might already have ideas of sub-goals and the detailed steps you expect to take towards the achievement of your main goal; if so, note these too. But don't be too concerned about producing a detailed action plan at this stage. There is a lot you already know about organization and your own needs, and clarifying your thoughts at this stage will assist your assimilation and application of new ideas and techniques, but you will also have the opportunity to refine your views as you go through the book, and we will review progress and plan the way forward in the final chapter.

BALANCING THE DIFFERENT ELEMENTS OF YOUR LIFE

Your life is made up of a whole variety of elements each competing for your time and attention, and it's easy to be side-tracked into one element to the detriment of others. A particular activity may start to take up more of your attention than anticipated, or an interesting issue may draw you away from other priorities. Take care to focus on the big picture and apportion your limited resources in a balanced way to ensure that you make progress towards all your objectives.

Whatever your job or lifestyle, there is likely to be a range of conflicting demands upon your time. So spend a few moments now considering adjustments you might make to the activities that take up your time and energy.

Ask yourself:

1 Are there elements of my life that are currently taking a greater proportion of my time and attention than they should? If so, what are they?

2 Why have they become excessively demanding?

3 What elements of my life should I be spending more time on?

4 What might I do to start adjusting the balance between these?

Try to formulate your answers to point 4 in terms of realistic objectives rather than vague intentions.

Determining day-to-day priorities

Life would be easy if, having planned the way forward, we could quietly and systematically pursue the achievement of our objectives. But it's seldom like that. In all probability, your day is spent responding to a multitude of routine chores, crises, requests and interruptions. In the face of this bombardment you need a means of determining which tasks will take priority. A simple way of looking at this is to define every demand upon your time,

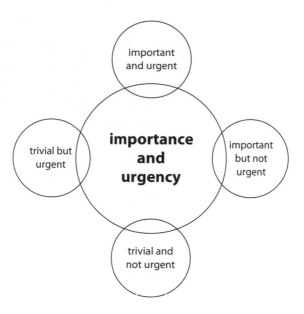

Figure 1.1 Determining priorities

whether it is self-generated or comes in the form of a request, in terms of its importance and its urgency.

The Second World War general and former US President Dwight Eisenhower was apparently keen on ordering priorities in this way, and reportedly said, 'What is important is seldom urgent and what is urgent is seldom important.' The principle of looking at time demands in terms of importance and urgency was subsequently popularized by Stephen R Covey in his book *7 Habits of Highly Effective People*, and has been widely adopted by time management practitioners. We can use a simple assessment of importance and urgency to categorize any task in one of four ways (See Figure 1.1)

Tasks that are important and urgent

Items that are both important and urgent are clearly the ones to which you must give the most immediate attention, but they are not always instantly identifiable. What constitutes 'important' can be problematic. A manipulative colleague may persuade you that what is important to him or her should feature just as highly on your agenda. Even worse, you may be the guilty party – convincing yourself that a minor diversion is an essential task that simply cannot wait. 'Important' in this context should mean important for the realization of your main objectives – not just those associated with your work, but wider, quality of life objectives too. If a balanced life style and family time have high priority for you, then getting to your child's first Christmas concert will rightly be just as important as anything your workplace can throw at you.

It's also worth questioning the notion of urgency. Once again it could be a case of other people's agendas rather than your own. It might be a matter of urgency that could have been avoided if you had planned your time better or if you had got down to work earlier rather than procrastinating. Some of us do our best work when spurred by a sense of urgency, but urgency that you control – where you set your own deadline or plan to work under time pressure – is a different matter from the sense of crisis and panic that comes from urgency that has crept up on you.

Tasks that are important but not urgent

These are the ones that generally present the biggest problems for those of us whose organization is not as good as it could be. They tend to be concerned with longer term objectives or major life quality issues and we need to ensure that we find the time to progress them. But often we are guilty of ignoring or postponing them, allowing other less important but superficially more urgent or attractive activities to take their place. Given inadequate attention, tasks of this type may suddenly be promoted to the extremes of the previous category (very important and very urgent) when a deadline looms or, in the absence of any meaningful deadline, may simply not get done. Such is the fate of many life objectives that are actually very important to us but are endlessly postponed until they wither and die. Plan your time effectively to reduce this possibility, and try to ensure that as much of your time as possible is spent on tasks in this category.

Tasks that are urgent but trivial

Needless to say, you should aim to ensure that such tasks don't draw your attention away from those in the previous category. Urgency doesn't make tasks any more important. Question why they are considered urgent. Often you will find it's no more than a gloss applied by others to justify their existence or cover their own inefficiency. On the other hand, you may be the main culprit, letting something that should be a simple matter of day-to-day routine build up to a point where it becomes pressing. In such circumstances it may be necessary to give consideration to your daily work habits, so that similar situations don't arise in the future. We will give some attention to how you might do this in Chapter 3. Where an urgent but unimportant task arises from somebody else's agenda, it may be a case of challenging the other person's perception of its importance, learning to say no to requests, delegating the task or running it quietly into the sand. Of course your decision on what to do may require an element of diplomacy. If your boss is the one asking, and he or she regards a particular task as important and urgent, then some adjustment to your own assessment may be necessary.

Tasks that are neither important nor urgent

You should not be wasting your time and energy on these. Frequently, tasks in this category are used as self-generated distractions – excuses for not getting down to other more important work that for one reason or another we view with some degree of apprehension. Recognize them for what they are and focus your efforts on tasks in the other categories.

The 80:20 rule

The 80:20 rule was originated by an Italian economist –
Vilfredo Pareto – around 1900. He discovered a consistent
phenomenon that about 80 per cent of the wealth of
countries was controlled by around 20 per cent of the
people. This 80:20 principle has since been expanded to
include all aspects of business and management – notably
'80 per cent of the results come from 20 per cent of the
effort'. The accuracy of this relationship may be disputed,
but the fact remains that, by concentrating your effort into
the important few actions rather than the trivial many, you
are liable to achieve more impressive results.

SUMMARY

The first steps towards better organization consist of:

- clarifying your current organizational strengths and weaknesses;
- identifying the reasons why you are currently not as organized as you might wish;
- building a positive belief in your ability to make progress;
- establishing a clear view of what you expect to gain from better organization;
- setting precise objectives;
- balancing the different elements of your life;
- determining day-to-day priorities.

ORGANIZE YOUR TIME

Time is unlike most other resources in that it is shared out equally. We all have the same amount of it each day. The differences between us lie in how we choose to spend it and how far we try to stretch it.

Your aim in managing your time better is either to reduce the number of hours you spend working, or to achieve more in the same number of hours. It is a matter of ordering priorities. When you say, 'I just haven't got the time for this', you are really saying, 'Something else is more important to me than this'. The problem is that, through inadequate planning and monitoring, we lose control of our schedule and fail to distinguish between the high pay-off and low pay-off demands on our time. We find ourselves saying, 'I haven't time for this' to an important commitment because we have already spent too much of it on trivia.

In this chapter, then, we will look at techniques for planning and tracking the tasks that we need to spend time on. First, however, let's consider how you currently spend your time.

HOW YOU USE TIME NOW

It is useful, before embarking on a new planning regime for your time, to give some attention to how you are currently spending it. Some time management programmes propose that you maintain a rigid time log for a couple of weeks. I don't see this as entirely necessary, but I do suggest that you carry out a simple monitoring exercise for a minimum of three days.

Monitoring exercise – task importance

The purpose of this exercise is to heighten your awareness of the relative importance of the tasks which go to make up your day, and to signal those areas on which you may concentrate your efforts for improvement. On a blank sheet of paper, draw three columns and label them 'Task', 'Time' and 'Assessment'. You might also like to make a few copies, as you will be using several of these sheets in the coming days.

Keep a sheet to hand throughout your working day and note in the left hand column every activity that occupies some of your time. Give a rough estimate of the time you spend on each item in the adjacent central column. It's essential that you are honest with yourself and include everything that goes to make up your day – the important and the trivial. An accurate picture of how you are currently spending your time is vital if you are to make progress in using this limited resource more effectively. You don't need to enter much information into the 'activity' column – just enough that you will remember what the item in question was.

At the end of the day, review your activity record and enter a number corresponding to the four categories of activity we encountered in the previous chapter:

1 Important and urgent

2 Important but not urgent

3 Urgent but not important

4 Neither important nor urgent

An example of how some of these entries might look is given in Figure 2.1

Task	Time	Assessment
Attending irrelevant meeting	2 hrs	4
Planning timetable for new project	30 min	2
Responding to urgent request for information	30 min	3
Preparing for tomorrow's progress review	1 hr	1

Figure 2.1 Monitoring task importance

Complete a sheet each day for a minimum of three days (preferably five) and compare them, asking yourself the following questions:

- Did I have any difficulty in distinguishing between those tasks that are important and those that are unimportant?
- If so, what steps do I need to take to remove this confusion?
- Roughly what proportion of my time is currently being spent on unimportant tasks?
- If this proportion is excessive, what could I do to reduce it?
- Was enough of my time spent on tasks which are important but not urgent?
- If the answer to the previous question is 'no', how can I increase time devoted to these tasks?

If, in the course of this exercise, you find yourself discarding or delegating tasks you would normally have carried out, that's fine. It's the start of organizing your time better.

It isn't always as easy as it might seem to distinguish between the important and the trivial, but your main reference point should be your objectives. Provided they have been well constructed, and you have taken care to break their achievement down into manageable stages, then tasks that conform to your main purposes should be quite readily identifiable. Where confusion remains, it may be necessary to re-examine and edit an objective or its constituent elements. There are, of course, different levels of importance, but I would suggest that initially you confine yourself to a simple important/trivial distinction. If you find this an inadequate means of prioritizing your time, you may wish to introduce grades of importance, but my advice would be to keep this as simple as possible (an ABC three point scale perhaps). Sometimes, despite your best efforts, a task which appears to be important subsequently turns out not to be so. Don't worry too much about this possibility. You can only make decisions based on information you have at the time.

Several of the possible strategies associated with reducing the time spent on unimportant tasks are outlined later in the book:

- Dealing with procrastination – later in this chapter
- Maintaining concentration – Chapter 3
- Delegating – Chapter 5
- Overcoming distractions and interruptions – Chapter 5
- Learning to say no – Chapter 5

Computer applications to assist with time monitoring

If you're looking for a more technologically driven approach to monitoring your activities, you might like to consider an application such as RescueTime (www.rescuetime.com). This web-based time management tool sits in the background and monitors your computer interactions, providing an analysis of the various applications, websites or documents you are using and offering an assessment of your productivity. If you choose to upgrade from the basic free service, it can also help you to track non-computer activity, as well as giving you the chance to voluntarily block distracting activities or to set yourself daily limits for certain types of activity and be reminded if you exceed them. Of course, what this application can't do, is make a judgement on the actual importance of the work you are undertaking. For example, you can spend an hour fiddling about on the word processor, and not producing anything of value, but RescueTime will still rate this time as very productive. So, while the application and others like it can give you an accurate reading of where your time is being spent, some input from you as to the importance and urgency of various tasks is still required.

If you don't like the idea of your computer use data being sent to a remote server, there are other, purely local, monitoring applications such as ManicTime (www.manictime.com) that fulfil some of the same functions.

PLANNING AND TRACKING YOUR TIME

Having examined how your time is currently being spent, the next step is to adopt a workable system for planning and tracking your time through the days, weeks and months ahead.

Planning

You need to be able to:

- determine your objectives;
- identify the steps needed to achieve your objectives;
- break projects and assignments down into their component tasks;
- decide how long you expect activities to take;
- decide when you will need to complete tasks over the coming days and weeks;
- identify what you will need from others in order that you can complete your own tasks.

Tracking

You need to be able to keep track of:

- your contacts;
- your meetings and appointments;
- what you have done and what remains to be done;
- who is doing what for you and by when;
- when you should follow up contacts and leads.

Planning your time

Effective planning requires that you take account of different time frames. The relative importance of longer-term and short-term planning will vary according to the nature of your work, but you may like to look at planning over three time frames. The first, and most general, might be an overall view of the next three months in terms of major objectives; the second, a week-by-week view to be sure that you are able to fit in the necessary preparation for impending commitments and deadlines; and the third, a detailed daily plan to ensure that you achieve a balance between important and urgent items and tasks which contribute towards longer-term objectives.

Planning your day

The time to plan your day is not first thing in the morning, but at the end of the previous working day. Once you get into the habit it will take no more than a few minutes before you pack up for the day. The task is completed while your brain is still in work mode and the following morning you are spared any indecisiveness and time-wasting while you gear yourself up for the day. You know exactly what you are aiming to do and you are able to hit the ground running. Resist the temptation to be overambitious in the number of tasks you set yourself, and don't book yourself up so heavily that there is no space for the unexpected. Crossing completed items off your list is very satisfying and helps to keep you on track, but resist the temptation to include too many easy hits on your list – small tasks which are there simply to be crossed off.

Mapping out your week

Just like daily planning, the time to map out your week is at the end of the previous week. You're not concerned with the same level of detail as for the daily plan, but you are aiming to establish an overall balance to your week, and to ensure that you are not caught on the hop. You will be thinking about what information you need to ask for on Monday in order that it is available for a task that must be completed by Friday; what you will have to do on Tuesday to prepare for that meeting on Wednesday; how much you will need to do each day to carry forward a major long-term initiative.

A regular Friday afternoon session when you map out the coming week is also a good time to review your work in the current week and give yourself credit for the things you have achieved. Don't succumb to frustration about the tasks you have not managed to complete. Use the session as an opportunity to ask yourself why they haven't been completed:

- Was there over-optimism on your part with respect to the number of tasks you allocated for the week?
- Did other important and unexpected work crop up that pushed some allocated tasks aside?
- Did something occur that made the tasks no longer necessary?
- Were you perhaps guilty of procrastination or avoidance?

Consider whether the tasks concerned need to be rescheduled and, if so, slot them into your upcoming plan using, as appropriate, techniques suggested later in this chapter to ensure they are achieved.

Overviewing the next three months

This is at a different level again from your weekly planning. It's about major blocks of time that will need to be devoted to projects and development tasks. The aim here is to ensure that deadlines in respect of different assignments don't clash, and that the timescales you allocate to major tasks are realistic. You are most likely to engage in this sort of activity in conjunction with planning a particular project.

If you are not currently in the habit of systematically planning your time, or your previous efforts to do so have been unsuccessful, I suggest you go for a weekly overview initially, in conjunction with a master list of 'to do' items (see later section in this chapter). Once you have a system of weekly time planning up and running successfully, move on to more detailed planning of each day and an increased awareness of the longer-term dimension.

Tracking your time

Tracking is about keeping on top of the activities you have planned – ensuring that you are reminded when actions are due, and monitoring your progress towards achievement of the objectives you have set yourself. The key to this is simplicity. Wherever possible, avoid recording information in multiple locations. This is an issue particularly if you are using paper-based means of recording commitments. Using a desk diary in the office and a pocket diary when you are at meetings and on the road is a recipe for overlooked appointments. If it is essential to have information in different formats, make sure that there is one master record. Limit the amount of manual transfer of information as far as possible to avoid oversights and minimize wasted effort.

Planning and tracking tools

The tools you use to assist planning and tracking may range from a notebook and diary to applications for smartphone or computer.

Choose those that best suit your preferred style and the nature of your work. Remember, too, that a poorly used tool can impede rather than enhance your effectiveness.

It may be that your needs are adequately served at the simple end of the range – a notebook to record tasks and general reminders, and a diary for appointments and timed commitments. All other tools are variations on this basic format, and increased sophistication does not always mean greater effectiveness. However, those of us with large numbers of contacts, tasks and appointments will want a more advanced means of tracking them. Let's look at the merits of paper-based and electronic systems.

Paper-based planners and organizers

Back in the 1980s no self-respecting professional would be seen without a leather-bound personal organizer, and a visit to an office stationery supplier today will reveal that while numbers and ranges have declined, there are still plenty around, produced in a variety of styles and prices. The basic format is a small ring binder with indexed sections containing pre-printed insert pages. Typical inserts available include:

- year planners;
- diaries in various formats;
- daily planning sheets – appointments and things to do;
- monthly objectives and project planning sheets;
- telephone and address book inserts;
- pages for notes;
- budget planning and expenses planning.

The idea is that all necessary working information is contained in one convenient folder. Users can switch their attention easily from a long-term to a short-term view and can swiftly update information wherever they might be. New pages can be inserted and redundant ones removed so that the organizer remains indefinitely expandable and always up to date. The downside is that there may be some need to transfer information from one page to another and some of the tools, year planners for example, are a little too small for serious use. Also, if you have a large number of contacts for your address book or need to make a lot of notes, you can find these sections becoming unwieldy.

Personal information managers (PIMs)

These computer applications are in effect customized databases for storing and tracking personal information. Many also serve as e-mail clients. The daddy of them all is Outlook, which comes packaged with some versions of Microsoft Office, but there are numerous other good examples, both commercial and free of charge, offering varied degrees of sophistication across the whole range of devices from desktop computers to smartphones. In some cases the software and associated data is located online, allowing them to be accessed from anywhere, or 'cloud' connectivity is employed to provide synchronization of data across multiple devices and the sharing of information between different individuals.

Typical contents of a personal information manager are:

- an address book to manage contacts;

- task lists which can be arranged under subject categories and may permit some simple project planning and tracking in terms of target date, person responsible, planned duration and percentage of the task completed;

- A calendar and appointments scheduler, which may be integrated with the address book and task lists, and which offers facilities for reminders and recurring appointments.

- recording of time spent on activities and expenses tracking;

- free note space which may be adapted to particular purposes.

> **Cloud Computing:** Internet based computing activity where elements of software and/or data storage are located at remote data centres rather than on the user's computer.
>
> **Smartphone:** Mobile phone that, in addition to basic voice and text facilities, has features found on a portable computer. Smartphones can connect to the internet, send and receive e-mails as well as performing a wide variety of productivity tasks through specialist software applications, commonly termed apps.

The great benefit of a PIM is the way that information can be integrated and viewed in different ways, without the hassle of manually transferring it. You can plan your activities within a project, and slot tasks into your schedule over a period of weeks taking full account of your other commitments. On the appointed date for commencement of a task, the 'to dos' will pop up and won't go away until you have signalled them as complete. Regularly recurring commitments only need to be entered once. You can view the big picture and the small and link people in the address book to assignments and appointments. Routine reference information or essential notes are easily incorporated, and it is simple to track time and cost. Depending on your software and sharing setup, you may also be able to assign tasks to others and be kept updated on progress, or to compare diaries online when seeking suitable times for a meeting. You do, of course, need a suitable device to hand in order to access all these facilities, although this is much less of a drawback than it used to be given the ever increasing sophistication of portable devices such as smartphones. These may even have additional facilities not available on conventional computer hardware. For example, those incorporating GPS capability can be set to give you a specific reminder when you are in a particular location.

The problem with small hand-held devices has generally been the difficulty of putting information into them. Smartphones tend to use either a miniature keyboard or a touch sensitive screen and virtual on-screen keyboard for data input, although increasingly there is also inbuilt voice recognition software. The keyboard options aren't particularly conducive to the input of large amounts of data but, for those who want to use their smartphone as an alternative to a laptop, there are folding keyboards that can allow for a near normal typing experience. However, such is the immediacy and reliability of synchronization services that, where significant amounts of data need to be input, it is frequently easier to carry out this task on desktop or laptop and synchronize with the phone.

What is best – electronics or paper?

It all depends on how you like to work. Paper-based systems are clearly much less powerful in terms of cross referencing, and require a degree of duplication. They lack the facility for automatic reminders and it's easy for items to get lost. On the other hand, inputting or extracting information from computer-based systems can interrupt the flow of other activities, and there may be new skills to learn. Neither should you underestimate the gizmo factor. If you're into gadgets, it's possible to get carried away by what your hardware or software is capable of doing, rather than what you actually need it to do.

There is no doubt that we are increasingly turning to technology to assist our personal organization, but it is not yet time to declare an end to paper-based methods. Even the most technologically committed of us will admit to tasks where we prefer to use paper – for example, when mapping out the activities to be included within a project before getting down to detailed planning. For my part, whilst I use the PIM software extensively, and synchronize the information it contains with my desktop PC, laptop and phone, I will always keep a notebook to hand, often preferring to make a scribbled note to be entered later rather than interrupt the flow of other activity in order to interact with an electronic device.

'To do' lists

Whether a 'to do' list is scribbled on the back of an envelope or flashes up on your computer screen, its essential purpose is the same, and so are its potential drawbacks. It can be a simple yet powerful tool or a meaningless exercise. The difference lies in how you apply it, and there are some important points to bear in mind if 'to do' lists are to work for you.

The first question is: where does your list come from? It's not going to be a huge amount of help if it consists of just a collection of items that pop into your head each morning. Such a list is likely to focus too heavily on attractive or urgent but not necessarily important issues. Your planning will benefit if you have some form of master list from which your daily and weekly lists are drawn. This is relatively straightforward if you have given appropriate attention to the long-term dimension of your activities – breaking down projects and major objectives into the tasks required to ensure their completion.

Separate your master list into different categories to keep it manageable and in order to be able to construct, edit and view a particular area of activity in isolation. Some PIMs come with pre-formatted categories. Get rid of the irrelevant ones, and set up new ones as the need arises.

Difficulty with 'to do' lists most often occurs as a result of unrealistic expectations of the number of tasks that can be completed within a given time period. Compiling a list of tasks provides a sense of getting to grips with one's workload and it's easy to become carried away. The consequence is a list that can be daunting and may feed a tendency towards procrastination. Stress about tasks not achieved replaces the positive buzz that compiling the list provided, and items on the list become almost permanent features – rumbling on from day to day and week to week until finally the whole exercise is abandoned.

So, it's very important that you build a habit of achieving the things you have listed. Keep your expectations reasonable and don't allow items to roll on day after day. Setting due dates for key tasks will help you structure your progress towards the completion of projects and major objectives, but allocating dates to every task at the time you first enter them in your planner or PIM can lead to logjams, with too many tasks from different areas of activity popping up at once. Your master list will be more manageable if you get into the habit of reviewing it regularly and setting due dates for less time-critical tasks in the week or fortnight before you expect to achieve them.

Activity

Before leaving this section, take a few moments to reflect on how you currently plan and track your time. What changes might you usefully make to the tools you are using at present?

SCHEDULING YOUR TIME – ESTIMATING TIME REQUIREMENTS

You start the day with, let's say, a dozen items on your 'to do' list. What confidence do you have that at the end of the day they will all have been crossed off? Not a great deal unless you have made some estimate of how long each task is likely to take, and fitted them in with the other commitments that make up your day. It isn't just about the confidence and credibility boost that comes from achieving what you set out to do, although that should not be underestimated. Estimating time requirements of tasks allows you to use the available slots in your day appropriately. If you have half an hour between commitments, you want, wherever possible, to fill it with a half-hour task. Discovering that a task you thought was going to take half an hour is really going to take an hour may result in additional time spent refocusing your attention when you eventually come back to it.

You will never achieve time estimation perfection. Tasks will contain unforeseen elements, and we all have a tendency to overestimate the time taken to complete those tasks we dislike, and to underestimate the ones we like. But taking a moment to think about what is involved with a task before you pop it into your schedule can greatly help the management of your working day.

Slotting tasks into the day

Your day is likely to be made up of fixed commitments – appointments and regular scheduled elements – and flexible ones – the tasks on your 'to do' list. Having roughly estimated the time you expect these tasks to take, you can then get an idea of when you will hope to fit them in. Don't seek to rigidly plan your whole day in advance, and don't spend a lot of time on the process. It should be a quick and simple way of giving your day shape and balance, fitting tasks into appropriate time slots, not a bureaucratic exercise. Half-hour time slots are a manageable way of dividing up your day, although for some smaller tasks you may want to think in terms of quarter-hour slots. Group several minor tasks – five or six phone calls for example – into a half-hour slot. Allow a bit of padding in your time estimates for some of the inevitable calls and interruptions. There is a great satisfaction boost to be had from completing a task in less than the time you expected it to take, but you also need to maintain your cool when tasks are taking longer than planned. Above all, stay flexible and deal with whatever the day throws at you.

Activity – improving your scheduling accuracy

If it isn't your current practice to estimate the time that tasks will occupy, start by setting a rough estimate alongside each item in your 'to do' list. Once you are under way, monitor the accuracy of your time planning for several days:

- Give a rough time estimate to every task on your 'to do' list.

- When you complete the task, enter the actual time taken alongside the estimate.

- Compare the differences over the period of a week.

- Are there any patterns of consistent over- or underestimation?

- Are there reasons you can discern for the inaccuracy?

- What can you do to improve accuracy?

PROCRASTINATION

Some element of postponement is both inevitable and necessary in a busy life, but we give ourselves needless stress and may greatly reduce our effectiveness if we engage in habitual procrastination. It's one of the biggest time management problems for many of us, and we need to take a look at why it occurs and what we can do about it.

The first thing to make clear is that procrastination isn't just about laziness or lack of resolve. If you view the habit as one which can be dealt with simply by showing greater determination, then you may well be disappointed. Many procrastinators find that resolutions to change their ways may work for a while, but then the bad habits start to recur. To achieve a more lasting response to procrastination we need first to understand the reasons for it. These may be complex and varied, and I have only the space here to give a brief outline of the possible causes, but let's look at some of the major reasons, starting with the most straightforward.

Dislike of particular tasks

Most of us have tasks that we would prefer not to be landed with. Whether it's general office housekeeping, keeping our finances up-to-date or responding to routine e-mails, we tend to postpone those we perceive as boring or bureaucratic until they have built up to the point that they cannot be ignored. By this stage completion may have turned into a major exercise, and this only serves to reinforce the sense of dislike, and to ensure that similar tasks will be the subject of further procrastination in the future.

Capacity for distraction

The ability to concentrate on the task in hand without resorting to self-generated diversions is an increasingly rare skill in our modern world. We know what we should be spending our time on, and we may even be relishing getting our teeth into it, and yet we experience a curious resistance. We seize upon any excuse to direct our attention elsewhere – checking e-mail inboxes, texting friends, engaging in aimless browsing or doing a bit of social networking. We tell ourselves, 'It will only take a couple of minutes to do this', but once the interruption has been made it leads on to other distraction activity, and half an hour is frittered away in the blink of an eye. In our modern environment, characterized as it is by an over-abundance of information, multiplicity of choices and immediacy of electronic communication, routes to distraction are much more prevalent than they used to be. The incidence of procrastination appears to be rising as a consequence. In a study carried out by the University of Calgary, it has been noted that the average self-assessment score for tendency towards procrastination has risen by 39 per cent in the past 25 years. The author of the study Professor Piers Steel says, 'It's never been harder to be self-disciplined in all of history than it is now.'

Desire not to offend

When faced with requests from others, most of us make an effort to be polite and helpful, even when the request concerns a task we would prefer not to have, or may not even be equipped to perform. A common and quite understandable response is to agree to the request but then to postpone execution, resulting in additional stress for the person accepting the task and frustration for the individual making the request. In such circumstances, it may be far better to take an assertive line, and say no to the request at the outset. We will examine how you might do this in Chapter 5.

Overly optimistic time assessments

Failure to gauge accurately the amount of time or work required to complete a task is a common problem that often accompanies a task we may be resisting for other reasons. A consequence is that we postpone commencement to such a point that the job cannot be fulfilled on time or its completion is rushed and inadequate.

Fear of failure

This is possibly the most prevalent reason for procrastination and the one least likely to be acknowledged. Many outwardly success-ful and confident people are plagued by a deep-seated fear of failure or of appearing foolish in the eyes of others. This is most generally the result of past experiences, and possibly insecurities generated in childhood. The anxiety about failing leads to a variety of responses:

- Catastrophizing – predicting the worst possible outcome from any proposed course of action, and allowing it to become a reason for inaction.

- Pretending to ourselves – inventing good reasons why the feared activity should not be carried out.

- Using other tasks as distractions or shields to prevent us having to face up to those that make us anxious.

- Setting hugely ambitious targets that have no realistic prospect of achievement, but where the perceived stigma of failure is much lower than it would be for a more modest target. If the individual fails, then he or she is able to take comfort in the knowledge that the target was close to impossible from the outset.

For those of us who fear failure, inaction can feel like a safer option than the anticipated pain of not succeeding. But the more we avoid those things that make us anxious, the greater the fear becomes. Initial avoidance eases our anxiety, and that leads us to employ the same strategy next time a similar situation presents itself. And by avoiding the things that make us anxious we give ourselves no opportunity to test the validity of our fears, so the exaggerations and distortions are reinforced. With each incidence of avoidance it becomes more difficult to face up to whatever we are afraid of. The difficult phone call, the confrontational meeting or the tough project that we have repeatedly postponed and worried about becomes almost impossible to contemplate. We are locked into a vicious spiral of avoidance.

Perfectionism

You might be surprised to see perfectionism in a list of reasons for procrastination. Surely a perfectionist is going to take pains to ensure that tasks are completed in a timely and effective manner. Undoubtedly, there are successful perfectionists for whom this is the case, but for many the opposite is true. People with a tendency towards perfectionism frequently place unrealistic demands upon themselves. They set the bar very high and then procrastinate over achievement of tasks. There is an underlying sense that if the high standards set are not achieved, the individual will be deemed less worthwhile as a person. Procrastination therefore becomes a tool to avoid unpleasant confrontations with reality. Where a task is postponed to the point that completion has to be rushed and imperfect, the individual is able to avoid uncomfortable judgements with excuses such as 'I could have done much better if only I had started sooner'.

These are just some of the reasons why people procrastinate. If you are someone whose personal organization is hampered by this habit, and many of us are, you need to give some attention to why it occurs in your own case. As with most problems, recognition of its existence is the first step to overcoming it. Keep an eye on any tendency to feed yourself excuses. Observe yourself over the coming days and look for any signs of resistance to particular tasks. Ask yourself what the reasons are – fear and anxiety, boredom, distractibility, perfectionism – the same ones will not always apply. Once you have identified the reason(s) it's easier to select the most appropriate strategies for overcoming the problem.

STRATEGIES FOR BEATING PROCRASTINATION

Once again I'm restricted in the amount of space I can devote to tackling this problem, but what follows aims to be a concise set of ten approaches that you may find useful in tackling this most stubborn of habits.

1. Don't fear fear

Recognize that it's OK to be anxious. Fears are made worse for many of us because we fear the very sensation of fear. We don't want to put ourselves in situations where we will encounter that sense of apprehension and discomfort, and so we stick doggedly to those things that we know will not put us in danger of it. But the experiences that make us afraid may also have the potential to offer us the greatest amounts of achievement and fulfilment, and the apprehension we feel before embarking upon them should be part of gearing ourselves up to give of our best. Most entertainers and sports people will testify to the fact that a certain degree of fear is a prerequisite to a really great performance. It's a matter of getting the balance right – a level of apprehension that brings out the best we have to offer and does not tip us into avoidance and paralysis.

Recognize too that you are the one who created these fears and anxieties, and that they don't exist anywhere other than inside your head. So, take ownership of them and acknowledge that what you have made you can overcome. Once you have made this attitude shift it is harder to invent excuses or to see your anxieties as insurmountable blocks placed in your way. Standing up to them becomes a matter of motivation rather than ability.

2. Get the pain balance right

The prospect of carrying out the tasks you are avoiding involves an element of perceived pain, but not doing them involves actual pain. The problem is that while the perceived pain is envisaged as a big hit – one that gets worse the longer a task is postponed – the actual pain of not carrying out the task comes in the form of a steady low-level irritation. You need to adjust the balance between the two, so that the pain of not doing the task outweighs the perceived pain of doing it. You can achieve this by: clarifying in your own mind the consequences of procrastination in terms of loss of control over your life, introducing penalties for non-performance, making a public commitment or opening yourself to be held to account for completion of certain tasks. Tackle perceived pain by noting the frequency with which tasks you have been avoiding turn out less fearsome than expected. Use this knowledge as a reference to help overcome future anxieties.

Similarly, address the pleasure side of the equation. What pleasure do you get from procrastination? The answer, generally, is none. How will you feel if you fulfil the tasks you are currently resisting? Focus on the end of a week in which you have achieved everything you set out to do, and visualize what completion will feel like.

3. Give yourself positive messages

The tendency to feed ourselves negative messages is most acute with those things that make us anxious or afraid. The prospect of tackling your fears becomes overwhelming if you are simultaneously filling your head with statements such as; 'I'm never going to manage this.' 'It's too scary.' 'Might as well give up now.' It's most important to approach feared activities in a positive frame of mind. If you think you can't do it then you can't. But just as negative self-talk diminishes your ability to act, positive affirmations can boost it. Choose some upbeat and constructive statements and mentally rehearse them at times you need to strengthen your resolve.

4. Use visualization

Visualization allows you to rehearse a situation liable to generate anxiety in a relaxed and controlled manner before the event. It's a technique best known in the sports arena. All top athletes and sports people use a tactic of mental rehearsal in which they visualize themselves achieving the standards they are training for. There is no doubt that it works, and can apply equally to other forms of human endeavour. Routinely picturing yourself succeeding at whatever you set out to do serves to remove psychological limitations you have placed on yourself, and it has been shown that during the mental rehearsal of visualization, two-thirds of the brain activity is the same as when the activity is carried out for real. Through it a positive mental image is created which counteracts the negative messages we have been inclined to feed ourselves and reduces the anxiety we might otherwise feel. We are enabled to approach the activity we have visualized with an attitude closely resembling that which comes from successful previous experience. Needless to say, this can have a potent effect on our performance and the way we feel about challenging situations.

Let's look at a typical example of a situation in which visualization can assist – a tricky meeting with a forceful individual in which you have to make a complaint, justify your actions, or administer a reprimand. Before you start, make sure that you are fully relaxed and untroubled by distractions or extraneous thoughts. You might want to investigate relaxation techniques if this is something that doesn't come easily to you. As you run the visualization you mentally rehearse all aspects of the interview – your confident body language right from the moment you enter the room, the eye contact, your tone of voice and the sorts of words you use. Picture yourself handling the situation successfully and assertively, and visualize the event as a dynamic enactment with you as the central participant. Don't ignore the anxiety that would be a normal accompaniment to such a meeting. Sense it, but visualize yourself overcoming it. You remain relaxed and in control, breathing calm and regular, no hint of becoming flustered. You are using the right words in the way that you would like to. Your body language demonstrates confidence and assurance. And perhaps most important of all, be conscious of the feelings you have about yourself. Recognize and appreciate the strong sense of self worth that comes with your assured performance.

Remember that visualization is a supplement to, not a replacement for, other preparation. If possible, run a visualization several times to make a real difference. Don't let any negative elements come into the picture – if they do, gently move them away. Don't dwell on them or seek to force them out, allowing anger and frustration to develop.

5. Reverse the order

Don't allow postponed tasks to build up a head of steam to the point where they become even more difficult to tackle. Arrange your list of things to do with the least appealing tasks at the top of the list and the ones you enjoy most at the bottom. Tackle the list in order and, not only do you get the relief that comes from overcoming challenges that otherwise might be postponed, but you are also rewarded with successively more attractive tasks as you work your way down the list.

6. Make firm commitments

As mentioned in the section on objectives, you should always ensure that what you set out to do is achievable. Anything that makes it onto your 'to do' list should be a firm commitment and not just a vague intention. Keep the list short to start with, and review what you have achieved at the end of every day and every week.

When you have resolved to tackle something you might be inclined to postpone, get on with it as soon as possible. The longer you leave it, the more you will find yourself inventing excuses for non-completion. Where the activity is not one you can deal with immediately, at least do something that commits you – arrange an appointment or schedule a time when you will deal with it.

7. Schedule tasks

Tasks that you don't like or are resisting demand a lot of mental energy just getting to the point where you're ready to tackle them. Often this is way out of proportion to their importance. You can greatly reduce this if you take action to ritualize tedious recurring tasks by including them at set times in your schedule until they become embedded routines that demand little mental energy. We will look at mobilizing the power of habit a little more fully in the next chapter.

8. Take controlled breaks

Tackle boredom by allowing yourself short controlled breaks at pre-determined times, or when a certain proportion of a task has been completed, but maintain your discipline to ensure the breaks don't become a distraction from the main task. If you need some help with this, there are various applications for phone and computer that can be set to remind you when to take a break and when to get back to work. A couple of these are mentioned in the 'useful tools' section of Chapter 8. For other examples, try entering words such as 'break reminder' into an internet search engine.

9. Record successes

It is very important to hang on to the sense of accomplishment that follows from successfully dealing with a task you have been resisting. Remember how different it feels from the temporary relief of avoidance. Note also how situations seldom turn out to be as difficult as you had feared. Keeping a diary may seem like a mundane activity, but it's a hugely valuable means of charting a way through difficult issues, reviewing progress and giving oneself positive reinforcement for a job well done. It can also be a valuable resource to draw upon if similar problems recur.

10. Make it easier

Rather than working through all tasks in a linear fashion, look for an easy point of entry to those where you have been unsure how to get started. The important thing is to make a start at whatever point.

Short bursts of concentrated activity – from five minutes to an hour – can work well as a way of overcoming inertia. They serve to overcome the psychological obstacle posed by a difficult or daunting task. You can amaze yourself by how much it is possible to achieve in just a few minutes and, if you punch holes in a task by this means, suddenly the task is no longer daunting and you are starting to achieve the momentum needed to carry you towards completion.

Similarly, divide large and complicated tasks into bite sized chunks so that they appear less formidable.

Activity – ask yourself

- What are the types of task over which I'm most likely to procrastinate?
- What reasons for procrastination might apply in my case?
- Which of these strategies can I use to lessen the extent to which I procrastinate?

MEETING DEADLINES

There are five main reasons why deadlines aren't met:

- The deadline is unrealistic to start with.
- The deadline is inadequately planned for.
- The person responsible for meeting the deadline is unable to get started on the task.
- The person responsible for meeting the deadline is let down by others.
- The person responsible for meeting the deadline spends more time on the assignment than necessary.

Dealing with unrealistic deadlines

The best time to counteract an unrealistic deadline is when it is being set. If you think that you are being asked to work to a deadline that isn't feasible, show that you have thought through the timescale rather than simply rejecting the proposal out of hand. Adopt a positive problem-solving attitude. Set out the stages that will need to be met in order to deliver on time, and explore whether there are any ways through the difficulty – such as additional resources which would help you to meet the required timescale – or whether it is possible for the deadline to be reconsidered. Unfortunately, deadlines are seldom set in a perfect working world, and while the timescale for a project may seem reasonable when viewed in isolation, the chances are that it will cut across other assignments that also have deadlines. One tactic you can adopt with the person setting the deadline is to ask them whether it takes priority over the other deadlines you are working to, and if so, which they would wish you to set back in order to meet the timescale on the new job. Remember too that some of the least realistic deadlines are the ones we set ourselves. Just as we pile too many activities into our daily 'to do' lists, so we overestimate just what we will be able to achieve in the coming weeks and months.

In some circumstances there may be deadlines that are unrealistic but not subject to influence. They may arise from the requirements of external bodies, regulators or clients. If affected, the only solution is to address the other demands on your time to free the space that will allow the deadline to be met. Once again, it is essential that you do this early enough to make a difference.

Before you start work, make sure you are completely clear what is required of you, what resources you have at your disposal, and what additional support you may call upon if necessary. Failure to deal with these issues is a frequent cause of missed deadlines.

Planning to meet your deadline

OK, so you have accepted the deadline. You now need to plan your implementation of it. Break the assignment or project down into a series of stages which will lead you to a successful conclusion and try to estimate the amount of time each will take. Calculate the number of working days between now and the planned completion date and ask yourself what you will need to do each week (or each day if you are dealing with a short deadline) in order to achieve it. Build in sufficient slack to allow for unexpected events and delays, and make sure that, in estimating the time needed for each stage, you have taken account of the other commitments which have a call on your time.

As you work towards completion of your project, use the finishing point for each of the stages as a milestone – a point at which you can monitor your progress, and ensure that you are on track. Use them also to give yourself the positive reinforcement necessary to maintain motivation. If you are able to get ahead of your schedule at any time, resist the temptation to slacken off. Use the time to build in some additional flexibility at the end of the project. The tidying up elements are often the ones most likely to be underestimated.

Inability to get down to the work

This tendency frequently accompanies poor planning. It may be that you are not sure you have all the information you need in order to make a start or just that the finish date seems such a long way off. You convince yourself that you have ample time and will be sure to get down to it in a day or two. People will often procrastinate over the start of a project because they lack confidence in their ability to succeed at it, or they are unsure where to start. If affected by this, then cast aside worries about tackling the task at the beginning, and simply pitch in at whatever point appears to be the most straightforward. The momentum you gain from making inroads into the task will usually outweigh any inefficiencies resulting from stages tackled out of order.

Avoid being let down by others

Often, completion of a project or assignment will not be entirely in your hands, and you will be reliant on input from others if you are to meet your deadline. Once again good planning is the key to ensuring that others don't present problems for you. Recognize that they will have priorities of their own, which are likely to differ from yours. Let them know in plenty of time what it is you require from them and the date by which you will need their input. It generally helps to set this date a few days before you actually need it so that any laxity on their part doesn't throw out the schedule for any subsequent work you need to do with their input. Make your requirements as clear as possible so as to avoid any misinterpretation.

Don't go over the top in seeking perfection

This is another failing which signals lack of confidence. It may be a matter of research or information gathering which is out of proportion with the task in hand and results in the person undertaking the task becoming bogged down and unable to see the wood for the trees. Or it may be unwillingness to let go of the project – relentlessly honing and polishing it with the aim of producing the perfect job. You need to avoid both these tendencies and recognize the point at which further effort does not produce a commensurate return.

Activity – ask yourself
- What difficult deadlines have I been faced with recently?
- What were the reasons for the difficulty?
- How do I need to change my way of working in order to address such problems in future?

TIME MANAGEMENT AND PROJECTS

I have referred to projects several times in this chapter, and it is worthwhile spending a few minutes considering the particular demands that projects place on your time. In the context of this chapter, we shall regard the term 'project' as including any undertaking leading to a significant outcome, where successful achievement requires completion of a number of elements over a period of time. It may be an assignment you carry out entirely by yourself, or may involve the input of others.

One of the major difficulties with project activity from a time management perspective is that it has to take place alongside other work. Harking back to the breakdown of work by importance and urgency which we used earlier in this chapter, it usually falls into the important but not urgent category and for that reason may be pushed off schedule by other, more urgent pressures which are actually less important. Care in planning and tracking your projects is therefore vital.

Whole books are written on project planning and management, and there are some complex techniques necessary for handling projects with hundreds of time-critical tasks, possibly involving the input of numerous individuals or organizations. This book, concerned as it is with personal organization, clearly cannot enter that level of complexity, but there are some basic principles that apply to all projects. Any project should embody five stages:

- initiating – clarifying general aims, setting out objectives;
- planning – breaking the project down into tasks and activities; deciding in what order they should be accomplished; determining the timescale, deciding what resources are needed;
  executing – carrying out the work, co-ordinating the input of others, resolving difficulties;

- monitoring – ensuring the schedule is progressing according to plan; redefining, rescheduling and reallocating resources as necessary;
- completing – finalizing the results, reviewing the outcomes.

The organizational skills required for successfully completing projects are largely those covered in other parts of this book – setting objectives, delegation, meeting deadlines, estimating time requirements – but you should give particular attention to defining tasks and the order in which they are to be carried out. This is something that requires you to ask a number of questions:

- What activities are needed to achieve this objective?
- In what order should they be carried out?
- Do any of them need to be broken down into smaller tasks?
- What resources are required to accomplish them?

The most common problem in defining tasks is a tendency to accept the first answers that come up. Don't expect, even with straightforward projects, to pull out all the answers at once. Revisit your first attempt. You are quite likely to see new elements that were not immediately apparent.

Depending on the complexity of the project, it may be necessary to identify sub-projects, each containing its own set of tasks and sub-tasks. Some tasks will be dependent on the completion of others, or may have others dependent on them. Delays in completing such tasks can throw out the whole project schedule, so it is important to clarify start and finish dates for them, and identify what room there is for slippage.

If you are planning a project which has a lot of interrelated tasks, project planning software can greatly facilitate the process. It will allow you to alter timings and relationships and to add or move tasks until you are satisfied with the project schedule. You can then make use of powerful charting and tracking facilities offered by the software. However, these packages are not simple and may involve a significant learning task if you are unused to project planning conventions. For this reason a PIM is to be favoured over free-standing specialist software for those projects that are not too complicated.

SUMMARY

If you are to organize your time more effectively, you need to:

- be aware of the way your time is currently spent;
- be able to plan your activity over different time frames;
- select planning and tracking tools that work for you;
- estimate the time required to complete tasks;
- work to reduce procrastination;
- adopt an organized approach to meeting deadlines;
- plan and track project activity.

UNDERSTAND THE WAY YOU WORK

After planning and prioritizing your work and taking steps to manage your time, the next point to consider is the way in which you set about it. In this chapter, we shall examine four features of your approach to tasks which can greatly improve effectiveness: scheduling tasks at appropriate times; working in short bursts to maintain concentration; mobilizing the power of habit; and dealing with decisions systematically.

SCHEDULE TASKS AT APPROPRIATE TIMES

It is likely that your workload consists of a variety of different tasks. You will have limited jurisdiction over when to carry out those that are dependent on the availability of others, but for the majority of tasks there will be some flexibility on timing. Most tasks will fall into one of three broad groups:

- *maintenance tasks* – those routine jobs which are essential to keep you functioning properly, staying informed, dealing with the normal inflow and outflow of information, organizing your workspace, completing routine correspondence;
- *people tasks* – negotiating, participating in meetings, persuading, reviewing performance, networking, resolving complaints, presenting, training, interviewing;
- *creative, planning and problem-solving tasks* – preparing plans and project briefs, writing reports, analysing information and drawing conclusions, finding solutions to problems, generating new ideas.

These are just a few examples. Depending on the nature of your job, there will be others appropriate to you.

Recognize the demands that different tasks place on you

Generally speaking, the maintenance tasks will make the most limited energy demands. Later in this chapter we will look at how many of them can be made even less demanding by harnessing the power of habit. Creative, planning and problem-solving tasks will normally require the greatest amount of concentrated attention and also larger blocks of time because of the need to get yourself up to speed before you are able to make significant progress. People tasks may be of long or short duration, but are frequently the ones which make the greatest demands on emotional energy. Those that may involve an element of confrontation are particularly draining. If you have several of these tasks, try tackling them together – one after the other. The head of steam you build up to tackle the first helps to carry you through the subsequent ones and, overall, you will find it less emotionally draining than having to gear yourself up for each one individually.

We are all familiar with the idea of a body clock which regulates our sleeping and waking. Anybody who has ever worked a night shift or crossed time zones will testify to the havoc caused by its disruption. But we give much less attention to the peaks and troughs of alertness that occur throughout our waking life, and which vary significantly between individuals. Needless to say, the alertness cycles in your day can have a potent effect on performance and it pays to schedule your most demanding tasks at the times you are best able to deal with them.

What are your best times?

We are accustomed to describing ourselves in general terms – 'I'm a morning person', 'I do my best work in the evening' – but have you ever looked at your work patterns in more than the most cursory terms? You may have become locked into a way of working not particularly suited to your body rhythms as a result of difficulties in organizing your day. You may assume, for example, that evenings are the times when you do your best planning and problem-solving activity, when in fact those tasks have been squeezed into that end of the day because you have found it impossible to give them the concentrated thought they require amid the distractions and interruptions of normal working hours. If, as a result of better organization, you are able to deal more effectively with interruptions, you may find that you can readdress your assumptions about the best times to take on particular tasks.

Start by examining the way you currently work with some simple analysis. Record your daily activity each day for a week. This can take the form of your daily 'to do' list, supplemented by those other routine activities that make up your day. Mark each item with three symbols:

1 a letter to indicate the type of task: 'm' for maintenance, 'p' for people, 'c' for creative;

2 a number between 1 and 5 to show the time of day you carried it out: 1 = early morning, 2 = late morning, 3 = early afternoon, 4 = late afternoon, 5 = evening;

3 plus or minus signs to indicate perceived energy levels: + + = high energy, + = moderate energy, – = fairly low energy, – – = very low energy.

At the end of the week, examine the outcomes to see whether there is any pattern of activity that warrants change. Are there intensive tasks you are currently attempting at perceived low spots in your day? Are there easy maintenance tasks that would more usefully occupy those low spots? Make adjustments to your schedule in the following week and note any improvements in performance.

Why you can't always rely on the same body rhythms

Your normal pattern of energy peaks is a good guide to the times when you should schedule your most demanding tasks, but don't regard it as infallible. On the days when you are slightly under the weather, or at the end of an exhausting week, there may be no appreciable energy peaks and any sort of demanding activity is a struggle. If you have any choice in the matter, don't labour on with a difficult task that is not working for you. In these circumstances you are unlikely to break through into sunny pastures. Far better to switch to a more routine maintenance task and return to the intensive one when you are rested and reenergized. Beware, however, of using this as simply an excuse for procrastination.

On the reverse side of the coin, when things are going particularly well, don't stop just because you have reached today's target. If you have energy and creativity to spare, and a task is flowing for you – go with it. Keep your schedules flexible and be prepared to listen to your body.

Fit the task to your available time

There are some tasks that you can only set about if you have a significant chunk of time – you need to gather resources around you, get yourself into the right frame of mind and make sure that you are free of interruptions. Other tasks you can dip in and out of more quickly. Don't waste your time trying to gear up for a long-slot task when you only have a short slot available. Keep some quick pay-off tasks handy for those spare moments when somebody due for an appointment is running late, when a meeting doesn't start on time, or while you are waiting for a train.

MAINTAIN CONCENTRATION AND MOTIVATION

Our capacity for sustained concentration will vary according to the nature of the task, the time of day and the degree of distraction, but even at the best of times it is finite. When tackling lengthy, mentally intensive tasks we need regular breaks that allow us to maintain our focus. But as we have already noted, it's easy to slip into disorganized habits, whereby breaks become diversions that take on a momentum of their own and prevent us getting back to the main task in hand. Successfully negotiate your way through lengthy tasks by adopting the following rules:

1 Make breaks short and reasonably frequent, but never take them on impulse.

2 Set yourself a succession of clear, timed targets, each with an element of challenge that is demanding but achievable, to see you through the overall task. A period of between 30 and 60 minutes for each target is generally the most workable. You may be able to concentrate on some tasks for a longer period, but for most attention will be on the wane after this time. A tough challenge to be achieved in an hour is less daunting than one that you expect to take two, and you're also less likely to cut yourself any slack. It's possible to blast away at a task for this length of time and achieve more than you thought possible.

3 The timed element to your target is important for a disciplined approach to the job, but go for the achievement of your target task rather than sticking rigidly to the time allocation. If you

achieve it in less than the target time, so much the better – give yourself a pat on the back. If it takes a little bit longer than you thought, then stick with it to see it through. Only if you find that a task is taking a lot longer than you anticipated or you hit a complete brick wall should you reassess your expectations. In such a situation you might set a lesser target to be achieved within the chosen time period, or look for a way of getting past the obstacle that has blocked your progress, perhaps seeking a different angle on the problem or moving to a new part of the overall task with a view to returning to the problematic area later. Do not permit an unexpected hitch to be an excuse for downing tools.

4 At the end of each target period, before you take a break, set your next target task and make a start on it for just a few minutes. That way, you will be returning to work in progress, and the effort of refocusing will be significantly less.

5 OK, you can take that break now. Just a few minutes doing something different is generally enough. It might be a quick and easy maintenance task, an undemanding phone call or an opportunity to stretch your legs or relax your eyes after a sustained spell of computer activity. What matters is that it should be different from the other task you have been doing, and you should not allow it to develop into a lengthy diversion. If other supplementary tasks arise, give them their own slot on your 'to do' list and get back to the main job in hand.

MOBILIZE THE POWER OF HABIT

You only have a finite amount of energy each day and you want to be able to expend it as productively as possible. But the chances are that all sorts of trivial and time-wasting tasks are using up your available resources and preventing you pushing forward those larger projects which require sustained concentration and effort.

By enlisting the power of habit, you can free up the energy you need to devote to the intensive tasks which will really make a difference to your effectiveness. If you pride yourself in bringing an element of creativity to your work and have an instinctive antipathy towards anything that smacks of becoming a creature of habit, console yourself in the knowledge that having some habits and routines in your day can give you more energy to tackle the creative things at other times. Routines are also valuable for dealing with boring tasks that you might be inclined to postpone.

Consider the routines you go through when you get up in the morning – cleaning your teeth for example. They have become ingrained – part of the way you start your day. Your thoughts are elsewhere while you are doing them – listening to the radio or planning your day – and you don't worry about them. They demand no mental energy. There are tasks in your working day which can be turned into the equivalent of cleaning your teeth. They may not permit quite the same level of mental detachment, but they're tasks which currently use up unnecessary energy. They vie with all the other demands upon you for a place on your busy schedule – you have to decide when to do them, and worry about them when they are not done.

A number of the general organizational tasks featured in this book may usefully be made the subject of habits and routines. They include:

- updating your schedules for the following day/week – Chapter 2;
- handling incoming information – Chapter 4;
- keeping your workspace clear and organized – Chapter 6;
- carrying out routine filing and computer housekeeping – Chapter 7.

There will be others specific to your job. On the flip side of positive habits which can free up our energies for more important activity are current negative work habits which condemn us to ineffectiveness.

Frances Craig is a classic example of someone whose workspace habits limit effectiveness. Although disciplined and organized in many other ways, she works amid overwhelming and distracting clutter. She is aware of the time she wastes looking for things among the heaps of material around her office and the overstuffed inbox on her computer, and she is conscious that with a little more discipline she could work a deal more effectively. She engages in periodic purges, during which important material is liable to get ditched with the junk, but so far she has not succeeded in building up a regular habit of workspace organization.

What fixes habits?

Habits, positive or negative, are fixed by repetition and reinforcement. Everybody is aware of the role that repetition plays in habit formation, but often we fail to persist for long enough to make a new routine automatic. We need to remember also that repetition will only work if it is accompanied by reinforcement.

Reinforcement can be positive or negative. Often overlooked examples of positive reinforcement include a word of congratulation (even if it comes from yourself) or simply the boost that comes from crossing an item off your 'to do' list. Negative reinforcement may come in the form of unwelcome discomfort. Some reinforcers are stronger than others. Those that are clear and immediate tend to have more effect than those that are vague and in the future. In the case of Frances and her workspace habits, the consequences of any different way of behaving are vague and indefinite by comparison with the immediate reinforcement provided by her current work habit, which she perceives as the ability to move quickly and easily from one job to another with the minimum of preparation or clear-up time. To change her behaviour she needs to make a deliberate connection between different habits and their consequences, and to work on reinforcing it every time she exhibits the desired behaviour.

Habits are also bolstered by your environment – including your own attitudes and perceptions of self, those close to you and the prevailing culture in your place of work. Frances's view of herself as a busy, creative type is a part of the background to her behaviour, as is the tendency in her organization to view a tidy workspace as an indicator of somebody with not enough to do.

It follows from all this that simply deciding you are going to introduce new routines into your working day is no guarantee of success. You need to address the environment in which your current behaviour flourishes, and work on nurturing and reinforcing the desired habits until they become automatic. It won't happen immediately but the end result will be worth a bit of persistence.

Activity – ask yourself

- Which of my current work habits contribute to effective performance?
- What are the work habits that limit effective performance?
- What new habits could I develop to improve performance?

Tips for changing habits

1 Start thinking in positive terms about the habit you are working to develop. Associate it with desirable outcomes – the chance to free up time and energy for creative and enjoyable jobs – rather than focusing on the boring and mundane nature of the task itself.

2 Similarly, associate new habits with positive aspects of your self-image. They are essential parts of your creativity and decisiveness rather than routines that bring out your bureaucratic traits.

3 Change the environment in which those habits you wish to change currently flourish. For example, coincide a change in desk organization with an overall purge on your workspace.

4 Remember that immediate positive reinforcement is what fixes new habits. This might come in the form of crossing an item off your 'to do' list, rewarding yourself with a desirable outcome (now I can go home, now I can go to lunch) or simply congratulating yourself on a task completed. Give yourself immediate positive reinforcement every time you engage in the new behaviour.

5 Hang your new routines onto key times in your working day. First thing, just before lunch, immediately after lunch, just before you go home. Associating them with constant landmarks makes them less likely to be overlooked.

6 Continue reinforcing and monitoring the new behaviour until it is established. Include the new work habit on your daily 'to do' list for several weeks and reward yourself for sticking to it.

7 Find ways of providing timely reminders for those newly introduced routines that will not occur on a daily basis. If you use an electronic means of managing your commitments, you might employ the recurring appointment facility to prompt you at the appropriate times.

8 Make use of checklists, forms and templates to reduce the mental effort involved in completing routine tasks.

9 Don't try to take on too much at once. Be satisfied with incremental steps, nurturing new habits until you are convinced they are established before turning your attention elsewhere.

SHARPEN UP YOUR DECISION MAKING

Decisions come before action. If you suffer from indecisiveness or poor decision making, it will inevitably have an effect on the quality of your personal organization. And if you are fussing over decisions that don't need to be taken or that could be delegated to somebody else, then you will have less time and energy for the things that matter.

There are a number of things that may get in the way of effective decision making:

- fears and anxieties;
- availability of information and other resources;
- conflicting timescales;
- the behaviour of others.

Fear

Fear, as we have already seen, is a factor in procrastination. Decisions are often postponed or referred elsewhere out of fear of making a mistake. Anxiety about the process of implementing a decision may be just as important as choosing the right course of action. You may know what is the right thing to do, but the prospect of carrying it out is frightening. Possibly it holds the prospect of unpleasant encounters with others. Difficult decisions to do with people – disciplinary matters, for example – are often bucked for this reason.

Information

Information is the cause of so-called 'analysis paralysis'. Either there is insufficient information to make an informed decision – often an excuse used to justify procrastination – or there is so much that the person responsible for the decision is overwhelmed. There is a fear element to information gathering too. On the one hand lies the fear that acquiring further information may throw up additional complications. On the other is the equally damaging fear that if you stop information gathering you may miss an essential nugget that would set you on the right track. You need to keep data acquisition in proportion to the importance of the issue to be decided, and learn to recognize the point at which you have obtained sufficient data to define and weigh the options adequately, without tipping over into additional work, producing rapidly declining benefits.

Timing

You don't need to be told about windows of opportunity. Making the right decision at the wrong time can be as damaging as making the wrong decision at the right time. Some decisions have to be taken quickly, and dithering will allow the moment to pass. But take care not to rush decisions which need careful consideration – perhaps because there are several steps to them, or because they have implications for other activities. There may also be short- and long-term dimensions to the issue you are considering. Biting the bullet in favour of a long-term solution is generally to be favoured over repeated sticking-plaster responses.

The behaviour of others

Decisions are not taken in a vacuum. For the most part they will impact on others who will come with their full quota of prejudices, hobby horses and baggage in the form of perceptions of status, role and reputation. They may need to be convinced of the benefits and perhaps to take ownership of the decision. Ignore all this and you might as well forget about making the decision at all.

A systematic approach to decision making

There are five parts to making any serious decision:

1. Clarify what you are about

This is best accomplished by asking yourself some questions:

- Why do I need to make this decision?
- What are the goals I wish to achieve?
- What information do I need to make this decision?
- What will happen if I don't do anything?
- Who do I need to involve?
- What is the timescale?
- What resources are available to me?

2. Identify the available options

This is a point at which short circuits often occur. In the process of identifying options, a superficially attractive one pops up and the focus moves away from exploration of all possibilities and towards justifying why this particular solution should be chosen. Even with decisions that require a speedy response it is worth taking a little time to ensure you have identified all the possible options before you start to evaluate them.

3. Weigh the pros and cons of each option

A simple approach is to adopt a balance sheet strategy for this task. Draw a line down the middle of a sheet of paper and, for each option, list the pros on one side and the cons on the other. Keep the goals of the exercise very clearly in front of you as you do this. Don't treat the pros and cons as if they all carry equal weight. You may want to give each a weighting on, say, a one to ten scale. But remember that you cannot expect to come to a conclusion simply by allocating and adding up weightings. Some points may have absolute rather than relative significance. A single point against may be of such weight that it eliminates all the points in favour. Beware also of what may seem to be overwhelming pros. The novelty value of some options may lead to the cons not being adequately explored.

4. Pare the options down to the point that you are able to make a choice.

Some options will have been immediately dismissed by failing to meet the goals or having overwhelming points against them. For those that remain, you need to take account of risk surrounding their implementation. How likely is it that factors beyond your control may affect the successful implementation of the decision? And what is the balance of risk against potential gain? Also consider elements such as how the decision will be sold to those who have to implement it.

5. Sell the outcome

Actually taking the decision may not be the point at which the job finishes, rather the point at which it starts. It is often then a matter of communicating the decision and gaining the commitment of others, and this is where a lot of good decisions come unstuck. Communicating the decision is a selling job and the principles of effective persuasion apply:

- Approach the task from your audience's point of view. Address their aspirations and fears.

- Establish credibility by demonstrating a clear plan for the implementation of the decision.

- Sell the benefits of the decision rather than dwelling too much on the reasons for it.

- Anticipate any objections that may be raised and prepare convincing responses to them.

Now move on

Recognize that you can never get it right all the time, particularly when there are people involved. At the time you make the decision, its implementation lies in the future. Circumstances may change for reasons you couldn't have predicted at the time you made the decision, and because of that you do need to keep the consequences of decisions under review. But having chosen the best option, you need to implement it and move on, without constantly revisiting the options to worry whether you have made the right choice.

SUMMARY

Effective organization of your workload will be improved if you are able to:

- recognize those tasks which place the greatest demands on you and schedule them when you are at your most energetic;
- fit the task to the time you have available;
- build up positive work habits and eliminate negative ones;
- take a systematic approach to decisions.

ORGANIZE INFORMATION

- Does the amount of incoming information you are required to deal with seem to be constantly growing?
- Do you find yourself going over the same material more than once without seeming to take it in?
- Would you like to be able to read faster at the same time as improving your comprehension?
- Do you have difficulty keeping up to date with the reading you feel is necessary for effective performance of your job?
- Do colleagues bombard you with forwarded e-mails, reports and copies of other written material that you don't need?
- Do you find yourself unable to decide what to do with documents and messages you receive?
- Do you put items to one side to be dealt with later?
- Do you retain magazines, reports and web references intending to read them, but never get around to it?
- Are you plagued by junk mail?

- Do you find difficulty locating a piece of information which you know is somewhere within a particular book or report?

If you haven't answered yes to any of these, then you are a pretty unusual being in today's workplace. Recent surveys have shown that throughout the developed world, people are struggling to cope with the vast quantities of information they are required to handle in their jobs and that widespread stress and productivity decline are a result.

In this chapter we will look at a systematic approach towards handling incoming information. We will examine ways to reduce the volume of what comes your way, and techniques to help you read, sort and assimilate it more efficiently.

IDENTIFY THE IMPORTANT INFORMATION

Some information is immediately recognizable as junk. Other items scream their importance. But it isn't always simple to separate with certainty the vital from the marginal. Use the following questions to help determine the value of whatever information comes your way:

- Does this information relate to a key element of my job?
- Would I choose to receive or keep this information if I had to pay for it?
- What is the worst that would happen if I ignored it?
- Is it information that I need at this point in time. If not, can I access it easily should I want it in future?
- Eighty per cent of the value comes from 20 per cent of the information. Is this item in the top 20 per cent?

You cannot be sure of getting it right every time, but resist the temptation to deal with this uncertainty by a strategy of 'if in doubt, treat it as important'. Information perfection – always having exactly the right information available at the right time – is not possible. While the availability of good information is important to the effective discharge of your job, more information will not guarantee better performance. Beyond a certain point, additional information will have a declining marginal value, and information has no value at all if there is so much of it that it cannot be properly interpreted and understood. So, recognize that you have no hope of taking in everything, focus on the important, and accept that your judgement will be imperfect. Remember also the need to discriminate between the urgent and the important. Items requiring a speedy response may assume a greater importance than they deserve. An unimportant matter which has been left unattended for several days does not become any more important because its deadline is approaching. It simply becomes more urgent.

ADOPT A SYSTEMATIC APPROACH

There is a common myth, perpetuated by some time management programmes, that every item of information should be handled only once. It doesn't work like that in the real world. For a variety of reasons, you might need to come back to a document. An item may genuinely need to be mulled over or put together with other information before you can make a sensible decision upon it. It may be more efficient to deal with some items in context with others on the same subject. What about the document or e-mail which makes you angry? Although a response fired off immediately may do something for your blood pressure, you are likely to produce a more effective reply, and one less likely to escalate confrontation if you wait until you have cooled off. Some items may need repeated handling in the process of drafting a complex document. If it is possible to touch a document only once, then this is clearly what you should aim for, but don't become too hung up on the 'one touch' approach. Ensure that no document or message goes back onto the pile, and that every item receives a positive action on the first touch. This action should be one of the following five Ds, summarized in Figure 4.1.

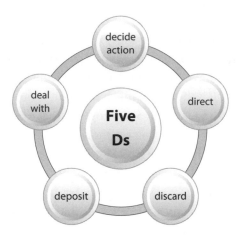

Figure 4.1 The five Ds

Discard

The quickest way to become bogged down with information is by wasting time and energy reading material of little or no benefit to you. So, the first question to ask yourself is 'Do I want this at all?' It should be quickly apparent if an item has no use for you, but we are often reluctant to consider the bin until we have waded through a document. There is also a tendency to put to one side documents that one is unsure about. There they form a mounting pile with other items, gathering dust or clogging up your inbox – occasionally being revisited in half-hearted attempts to clear the backlog. Remember that most information has a limited shelf life. A useful rule of thumb is – if it doesn't seem valuable today it isn't likely to tomorrow.

Deal with

Provided that you are able to do so quickly and effectively, you should deal with items when they first come to you. An immediate action on a document is satisfying and stress-relieving. It also means that you will not have to spend time refreshing your memory before you can act upon it in the future. Where it is not possible to deal with an item immediately, then at least decide what action you will take and when.

Decide future action

When dealing with paper, never return an item to the pile. Make sure you have a system for bringing forward items on which you will need to act, and make a point of noting the action required, or the possible options, on the document or a sticky note attachment. A concertina file marked with the dates of the month makes a useful 'bring forward' device. Place the item in the compartment corresponding to the date when you wish to revisit it.

Depending on your software, you can adopt a similar approach with e-mail. If you're using an application such as Outlook with a 'flag for follow up' facility, you can simply tag the message and choose when to receive a reminder about it. Other applications may not have the ability to issue timed reminders, but they will generally have some facility for flagging or tagging messages. Designate one of these tags for follow up, and you can easily run a search to call up all those messages you need to return to. Remember to remove the tag once you have dealt with the message. Alternatively, you can set up a special folder for all messages that have actions pending, but you must remember to visit it regularly.

You will need to exert some discipline in respect of items marked for future action:

- Do not use it to avoid one of the other four Ds.
- Do not move items on beyond the day you have originally set for action.
- If you have a 'to read' file, don't let it become a general dumping ground.

Direct

Don't send items to others just to get them off your own desk or out of your inbox, or because you don't know what to do with them. You will only add to other people's information burden, further belabour the internal communication system and possibly fill the bins of others more quickly than your own. Think about why you are redirecting the item and what you want the other person to do with it. A brief note will help them to assimilate and act upon it more quickly.

Deposit

Storing an item in whatever form of filing system is not an action to take because you don't know what else to do with it. Be sparing in what you file. This particularly applies to the filing of paper documents which tends to be labour and space intensive. You can afford to be more generous in the filing of digital documents, but even here a general policy of retaining material just in case can lead to more protracted retrieval tasks. We will look at ground rules for filing in Chapter 7.

AVOID OVERLOAD

However effective you become at handling the stuff, you will not achieve all that is possible unless you also take steps to reduce the volume of information that daily competes for your attention. Even if you only glance at the majority of it, you may be wasting considerable time and effort.

There is a tendency to feel powerless in the face of a relentless flow of documents, e-mails, calls, texts, web links and the like. But there are things that can be done to retain a greater degree of control.

The first step harks back to Chapter 1 of this book. If you are to have any hope of separating the wheat from the chaff, it is essential that you are clear about your objectives and can differentiate between the important and the trivial. Once you're able to do this there are several ways in which you can set about reducing your overload. Here are some possibilities.

Opt-out

It's hard to do business online without divulging e-mail addresses, but you should at least take care to ensure yours are not spread more widely than is necessary. When signing up for a product or service, check the organization's privacy rules to ensure that they are not going to divulge your address to other parties. Often there is an unobtrusive check box allowing you to opt out of on-going contact such as newsletters, updates and offers from associated organizations.

Don't circulate your mobile phone number too widely, especially to organizations that may use it to bombard you with promotional texts and calls.

Examine the range of printed periodicals, newsletters and online journals you receive and consider unsubscribing from all those that have offered only limited value in recent months.

If interactions with social networking sites are a factor in your overload, ask yourself some serious questions about the place of this activity in your life. There is an addictive quality to this sort of connectedness that can get out of hand. Is it imposing unduly on your working life? How genuinely important to you is the minutiae of other people's lives? Are you using it as a shield to avoid other tasks?

Filter

When searching or browsing for information on the internet, remember that you cannot possibly handle more than the tiniest proportion of the available information. Much of what is out there will be of poor or dubious quality, requiring further effort to interpret it or verify its reliability. Therefore, stick with quality sites. There will be further tips on assessing quality in Chapter 8.

Make certain that you are using the junk mail filters included with your e-mail or antivirus software as fully as possible to eliminate total junk and malicious mailings.

For those using RSS feeds and news alerts, use filtering options such as Google Alerts to ensure that only the things you really need to know get through.

Disconnect

Constant connectedness is a very serious impediment to effective working, and can greatly add to your sense of overload. One of the great benefits of most modern forms of communication should be their time independence. We should have the ability to choose when to respond to e-mails, texts and voicemail messages, but many of us handle them in the same way we would an old-style landline call – reading and responding as they arrive and disrupting other activity in the process. Restricting the number of occasions during the day when you will read and respond to messages can provide a major boost to productivity. We will look further at how you might take more control of this area of communication in the section on overcoming distractions and interruptions in Chapter 5.

Delete

Recent global estimates indicate that more than 70 per cent of e-mail is spam. However, by no means all unsolicited mail is total junk. A fair proportion is likely to be from organizations you have dealt with previously and indeed may do so again, but it is mail that you neither need nor desire at this particular time. Nevertheless, the inclination is to read it and possibly even retain it just in case. The demand on your time occasioned by each incidence of communication is small, but together they can add up to a large imposition. If you are struggling with the volume of incoming mail, hitting the delete button straight away is likely to make a deal more sense. Anything of value is liable to be the subject of further communication. Indeed, you can expand this approach into a general one of ignoring and deleting most incoming information unless there appears to be a good reason to do otherwise.

Cooperate

Remember that clear requests are more likely to get clear answers. If you are bogged down by an overabundance of forwarded messages or garbled communication, it may be that you haven't specified clearly enough what you require from others.

When you're not sure what to do with a document or who may need sight of an e-mail, the easiest solution is to engage in multiple copying and send it to everybody who might conceivably have use for the information therein. You have achieved two things – the offending item is off your hands, and you have also absolved yourself from any responsibility for failure to communicate. However, you have added to the information burden of others and have not necessarily communicated anything of value. If you aim to protect yourself by over-copying to colleagues, they are likely to respond in the same way.

There may be instances where several members of a workgroup can cooperate to relieve their collective information burden. If, for example, you all regularly have to read and assimilate complex documents, it may be possible to take it in turns for one lead reader to provide a summary for the others, thus speeding and assisting their assimilation of the document.

READ MORE EFFICIENTLY

The speed and efficiency with which you can assimilate incoming information is a significant factor in your ability to organize your workload. It has been estimated that people in information-intensive jobs may spend up to a third of their working day in activities involving reading, and yet most of us are not as efficient readers as we might be. The average reading speed is between 200 and 250 words a minute. With some simple techniques and practice this can easily be raised to 500+ without detriment to your understanding. Slow reading speeds are not particularly a function of education or intelligence. Many able and well-educated people read at or below the average speed. Even if you already read quickly, there is generally scope for improvement. It is a myth that only by reading slowly can we expect to understand material. Better comprehension can go hand in hand with faster reading.

What is my current reading speed?

If you want to estimate your reading speed, simply choose an appropriate passage, at least a page in length, that you haven't previously read. Try to read it at a normal pace consistent with understanding the content, but take an accurate note of the time it takes you. Next, estimate the length of the passage by multiplying the average number of words per line by the number of lines it contains. Use the following calculation to estimate your reading speed in words per minute.

$$\frac{\text{number of words in the passage} \times 60}{\text{time taken in seconds}} = \begin{array}{l}\text{reading speed in} \\ \text{words per minute}\end{array}$$

Why do we read slowly?

When we read, our eyes do not move continuously across the page, but rather hop several words at a time through the material. It is during the stationary period (fixation) at the end of each hop that the reading occurs; and it is, of course, the brain which does the reading rather than the eyes. In simple terms, we might think of the eyes as a still camera taking a series of shots which the brain then interprets. The main reasons for slow reading speed are:

- limited number of words encompassed in each fixation;
- fixations of longer duration than necessary;
- involuntary or deliberate back skipping over material already read.

A fourth factor in slow reading is a tendency to mentally hear the words as we read. This is known as sub-vocalization and is believed to originate from the approach used when we first learn to read – actually speaking the words aloud. The problem with sub-vocalization is that it restricts us to little more than the speed of the spoken voice, which is typically around 150 words a minute. Sub-vocalization can be greatly diminished if never entirely eliminated.

Training yourself to read faster is a matter of technique and practice. There are numerous books and courses available on the subject, and in the space available here, it is only possible to introduce a few techniques. With a little perseverance these should bring about a significant improvement.

Using a pacer

Most speed-reading programmes advocate training with some form of pacing technique which forces your eyes to move on and eliminates lengthy pauses or back skipping. You can use your index finger or the blunt end of a pencil, moving it swiftly across the page just below the line of text you are reading. At the end of the line, move the pacer quickly to the start of the next line, and so on. Maintain a pace above that which feels comfortable and refuse to allow your eyes to go back over what you have already read. Try softening your gaze to take in more words at each pass and make use of your peripheral vision. At first you may feel that you have taken in little or nothing of what your eyes have passed over, but with practice you will find increased levels of comprehension as well as speed. It has been shown that faster readers actually understand more because they are able to tune in to the general thrust of the piece they are reading, whereas slower readers become bogged down in detail.

It is natural to feel some anxiety about the process of taking in larger blocks of material at each hit, but in many aspects of our daily lives we absorb significant blocks of information at a glance. We register road signs, hoardings and headlines without stopping to 'read' them and we can significantly increase the span of words which we take in on each fixation. It is commonly thought that fast readers read down the middle of the page and that their span therefore encompasses the whole line of text. This is, however, very difficult to achieve except with text in columns. Fast readers may take in six or more words per fixation, and their eyes will remain in the central third of the page rather than following a line down the centre of it.

As your reading speed increases, you should find yourself able to progress to a smooth zigzag movement of the pacer, taking in more than one line at each pass, and without the necessity to lift the pacer from the page (Figure 4.2). Avoid reaching the point where you are forcing yourself along and are more conscious of the process of reading quickly than of what you are taking in. Once you have reached a reasonable speed you may wish to relinquish your pacer.

Figure 4.2 As speed increases, adopt a smooth zigzag motion with the pacer

OTHER TECHNIQUES

Increasing your reading speed will, of course, take a little time and you may wish to tap into the structured practice of a speed reading course. Whether or not you choose to do so, here are some further techniques you can employ almost immediately to improve both speed and understanding.

Preview for increased understanding

We read much more quickly and effectively if we are slotting information into a known framework. A few moments spent establishing that framework can pay significant dividends. The approach which follows assumes you are setting out to read a substantial document such as a book, periodical or report. It can be adapted for shorter documents and applies as much to electronic documents as paper ones.

1 Before starting on the main text, skim through the Contents page, Introduction and Summary (if there is one) or Conclusions.

2 Next, zip through the document, establishing an appreciation of the main structure and argument. Look particularly for section or chapter summaries. They are excellent for getting quickly to the guts of a document. Failing that, read the first and last paragraph of each section or chapter. These will often introduce and summarize the arguments contained therein.

3 Now, when you move to read the document properly, you will be filling in the gaps rather than starting with a blank sheet. You will know which are the parts you need to concentrate on, and which you can blast through or skip altogether.

Vary your pace

It goes without saying that texts vary in their levels of difficulty, but many people maintain the same pace regardless of what they are reading. Even within a document there will be some sections which are more difficult to absorb than others. Don't be afraid to slow down where the text requires it, and to power through the easier passages.

Focus on what is important

At some point in most documents there will be digressions from the main argument, things which you already know, things you don't need to know and straightforward padding. The best way to approach any reading task is with the question 'What do I need from this?' foremost in your mind. You will read more quickly and remember more, if you can focus on the elements which are necessary for you in whatever task you have to fulfil. Don't approach the printed word with too much reverence. The writer does not necessarily know any more than you do on the subject.

Develop scanning techniques

When you need to find a particular piece of information, you can move to it quickly by scanning. Focus your attention solely on the information you wish to locate and let your eyes follow your finger as you run it rapidly down the centre of each page from top to bottom. This process should be considerably faster than your paced reading, and if you are focused on the information you want to locate, it should leap out at you when you get to the relevant part of the document. You will improve with practice. Of course, scanning is no substitute for using an index where one exists. Scanning is generally unnecessary when seeking specific information in an electronic document. It is quicker and more reliable to use the search facility, entering a relevant word or phrase.

Be selective about what you read

Never try to read everything that lands on your desk or in your inbox. That way lies madness. You need to be ruthlessly selective and stick to those things which add value to your role. And remember – people who put reading matter aside for an indeterminate time in the future when they will be less busy are destined to be forever disappointed.

Catching up with reading

Catching up with reading is not a task that imposes itself on your schedule and consequently the pile just grows. Use the suggestions from the previous chapter to find a low-energy time in your week when you can build in a regular reading catch-up session. Provided you keep it fairly short and don't have unrealistic expectations of what can be achieved in each session, it can serve as a useful and rewarding variation on your other activities, and one that will not overly disrupt your flow or general productivity. It's important for motivation that when you turn to your reading file, you are not confronted with a teetering stack of dust-covered volumes or a daunting array of online documents. So have a ruthless clear-out before you put your new system into action. Ditch the less-relevant material and any periodicals more than six months old, so that you can start with a task that is manageable. Keep an easily transportable reading file to hand for those occasions when you are travelling by public transport or waiting for the commencement of a meeting that has been delayed.

READING FROM ELECTRONIC DISPLAYS

For a number of years now it has been accepted that reading from a screen is generally less efficient and more wearing than reading from the printed page. Studies in the past have shown that we are on average 25 per cent slower when reading from a monitor and have greater difficulty understanding what we read. When proofing documents on-screen there is an acknowledged tendency to miss errors that would be readily spotted on paper. Such difficulties with on-screen reading have been attributed to the lower resolution at which computer monitors display text and the fact that on-screen fonts tend to have a more ragged edge than printed ones, which the brain finds more difficult to interpret. In recent years, however, there have been huge advances in monitor quality and in the design of fonts specifically for on-screen reading, as well as entirely new displays such as e-book readers and tablet computers that aim to give a natural reading experience. Nevertheless, studies still indicate slightly slower reading speeds from electronic displays, and while users surveyed report the experience of e-book readers and tablets to be as enjoyable as reading from paper, most continue to find computer monitors less satisfactory.

It's possible that differences between our experience of reading from paper sources and electronic displays may not be entirely physical. We tend to give on-screen text a more cursory treatment, and one psychological factor behind this is frequently the reader's awareness that an internet page is perhaps one of millions competing for his or her attention. The consequent sense of not knowing whether this is the page offering the 'best' information makes for a tendency to flit through a document rather than committing to it.

USE YOUR MEMORY

The value of what you read declines pretty rapidly if you can't remember it. Fear of forgetting results in a number of negative habits. We hang on to documents of minor significance, read slowly and back skip over the printed page. For effective information handling we need to trust our memories. The more we use them, the more reliable they will be. If you do nothing to assist your memory you will forget up to 80 per cent of what you read within 24 hours of reading it. Here are a number of simple techniques which can help you remember better:

- **The level of recall you require will vary.**
  For some information, it will be sufficient for you to remember simply that it exists and where to find it. With other information you will need a grasp of the general subject and main ideas. At the highest level you may need to recall information in detail or even verbatim. Assist your memory by selective reading and awareness of the level of recall you need.

- **Read with a question in your mind.**
  What do I want to achieve from this? How does it fit into what I know already? All learning and remembering is a process of association.

- **Try to see the overall pattern to what you are reading.**
  We remember much better if we can see the general structure and the broad ideas into which the detail fits.

- **Use the information in some way.**
  Summarize it in your own words, make margin notes as you read, communicate the information to others, or act on it.

- **Recognition, the process of remembering with assistance from an external stimulus, is much easier than pure recall.**
  Make conscious associations which will help you to pull detail from your memory. It has been shown that the more bizarre the association, the more likely it is to work. Silly mnemonics, ridiculous visual associations, they all work.

- **Review important information to fix it in your long-term memory.**
  You will gain the most advantage by quickly reviewing material shortly after acquiring it (10 to 15 minutes) and again a day later. Experts recommend further review after a week and a month for reliable long-term recall.

Figure 4.3   Level of recall

SUMMARY

Dealing effectively with information is a matter of:

- separating the important information from the junk;
- maintaining a systematic approach with all incoming information;
- handling all incoming information as sparingly as possible;
- taking steps to reduce information overload;
- building up your reading speed and comprehension;
- using memory techniques and review to assist your recall.

ORGANIZE THE WAY YOU WORK WITH OTHERS

Much of our working day is spent in some form of interaction with others. The way you approach these interactions can have a considerable impact on your effectiveness. In this chapter we shall look at meetings, delegation, overcoming distractions and interruptions, helping others to be more organized, and learning to say no.

A STRATEGY FOR MEETINGS

The time-wasting potential of meetings is immense. In many organizations you can spend hours every week in meetings that achieve very little. But for all that we moan about them, we keep on holding the things and attending them. Why?

People go to meetings for reasons other than to make decisions. Meetings cultivate a sense of one's importance – closeness to the wheels of power. They are an opportunity to make an impression on your colleagues. Not being invited may smack of exclusion. I have known people, left out of meetings that had almost negligible relevance to them, become incandescent over what they perceived as deliberate downgrading attempts. There is also a social element to meetings, and they can be less demanding than some other forms of work activity. Once you are in the meeting you're cocooned, safe from phone calls, interruptions and the tough problems that inhabit your inbox. OK, so meetings are boring, but you can play a few mind games with colleagues or just let your attention wander.

Why do we hold meetings? Meetings are held to:

- impart information;
- elicit views;
- provide updates on progress;
- stimulate new ideas;
- work collectively on joint projects;
- motivate a group;
- plan strategy;
- reach decisions.

There are more effective ways of passing on information than dragging people together into a room and subjecting them to one of those verbal memo meetings where only the senior person speaks and everybody else sits mute. There are also non-meeting ways of consulting and eliciting views. The creative or brainstorming meeting has long been seen as a way of exploring new solutions to problems, but studies have shown that frequently people are more creative when working individually. Similarly, one-to-one reinforcement and coaching can often achieve more than a motivational team meeting, and the non-challenging culture ('groupthink') developed by some meetings may not favour good decisions.

So, in the face of all this, whenever the prospect of a meeting comes up, the first question to ask yourself is: Do we need a meeting at all? Unfortunately that question isn't asked often enough. In many organizations, meetings go ahead at regular intervals regardless of whether they are really needed. Business expands to fill the agenda and you have all the ingredients of a classic talking shop.

Assuming that you decide a meeting really is necessary, what can you do to ensure that it achieves its purpose without devouring too much of the participants' time? Unproductive meetings generally fall down on aspects of planning and management.

Inadequate planning

There may be no agenda, a poorly prepared one, or no clear purpose to the meeting. Information needed to make sensible decisions may not have been produced, or participants may have failed to read papers provided in advance.

Poor management

There may be inadequate control of timing, failure to keep discussion on the agenda, inability to control people intent on riding their pet hobby horses, inability to draw conclusions out of the discussion.

Here are some pointers aimed at overcoming these and other meeting problems.

Ten points to remember when calling a meeting

1 Frame the agenda as clearly as possible. Identify the specific questions the meeting needs to address rather than setting open-ended topics.

2 Indicate a target time allowance for each agenda item and stick to it as closely as you can.

3 Limit attendance to those who have something to contribute on the matters under discussion and the authority to implement decisions. Generally speaking, the more people there are at a meeting, the longer it will take.

4 Schedule meetings immediately before lunch or at the end of the day. People's anxiety to get away will override their verbosity.

5 Try not to schedule meetings in your own work area. You will find it harder to get away from any post-meeting hangers-on.

6 Start the meeting at the scheduled time. Waiting for late-comers encourages them to repeat the misdemeanour and irritates those who have arrived on time.

7 Don't allow discussion to be sidetracked onto matters not on the agenda. If they are important they can be dealt with at a subsequent meeting.

8 Don't waste time discussing matters where there is inadequate information to make a decision. Agree responsibility for obtaining and reporting the necessary information and postpone the discussion to a future date.

9 Avoid the practice of Any Other Business at the end of meetings if at all possible. It is often used by people too lazy to prepare an item properly for the agenda, and can result in bad decisions made on the basis of inadequate consideration. It can also kick into touch all your efforts at timing discussion.

10 Ensure that as soon as possible after the meeting, a record of the outcomes is prepared. The quicker it is done, the easier the task. Detailed minutes are generally unnecessary, and only give people something to argue over at the start of the next meeting. Action notes are more useful. They should include: a) what the meeting agreed; b) who has responsibility for actioning those agreements; and c) dates by which they should be actioned.

Ten points to remember when attending a meeting

1 Make sure beforehand that you know what the meeting is aiming to achieve. If the aim doesn't seem clear, question the convenor about it. This should have the effect of clarifying objectives, leading to a more productive meeting, or demonstrating that a meeting isn't actually needed.

2 Ask to be excused any meeting which does not appear to have any relevance to you. You have to be wise to the politics of this. If your boss is the one calling the meeting, diplomacy may require that you go. Often, however, the convenor simply hasn't given sufficient thought to meeting membership. Questions like 'What are you hoping I will be able to contribute?' can lead them to think again.

3 If only one item in a meeting is relevant to you, ask whether it can be placed near the beginning of the agenda so that you can be spared the rest of the meeting. Be aware, though, that this tactic sometimes sparks a bidding war on the part of others similarly affected.

4 Always read the agenda and any papers before a meeting and, without taking up an inflexible position, clarify your thoughts as to what you would like to achieve from the meeting.

5 If you expect your arguments to meet with some opposition, a little subtle lobbying in advance may be useful. Other participants may not have given the meeting much advance thought, and people are more inclined to stick with a view that they take into the room than they are to be won over by something they hear during the meeting. Handle lobbying carefully though. If the other person sees your approach as an attempt to exert undue influence, you risk actually turning them away from your point of view.

6 Think in advance about what you will settle for if you don't get what you want. Most people will not have thought about a fallback position. Skilfully presented – that is before it is

apparent to everyone that you have lost the argument – it can be a disarming way of getting at least a substantial part of what you want.

7 Don't overcommit yourself. Meetings are a bit like auctions. In the to and fro of discussion it's easy to get carried away and make undertakings you later regret. There's a natural wish to make a good impression in front of colleagues, but don't let yourself be tempted into taking on too many responsibilities or offering unrealistic target dates for completion of work.

8 If you find yourself locked into excessively long meetings, arrange for an 'important' appointment, or vital interruption, which will require you to leave before the end. Don't do it too often, or you will arouse suspicions.

9 You can help a weak chairperson by summarizing the arguments of others and pulling the threads of a discussion together to facilitate decisions. By all means draw people's attention to overruns on time, but take care to ensure that you are not a guilty party. We tend to overestimate the time that other people have been talking and underestimate our own loquacity.

10 Try to set some regular times when you are available for meetings attendance and make them known. If you are able to make this work, it can help prevent meetings breaking up your working week in such a way that you are unable to get to those tasks which require concentrated activity over a number of hours.

Alternatives to meetings

As noted at the beginning of this section there are better ways of doing some of the business that is traditionally reserved for meetings. Too often a meeting is the default response – the lazy option for dealing with an issue, and one that may occupy many more person hours and be less effective than an alternative approach.

It may be possible to achieve the desired ends without having to bring a group of people together in one place or adopting a 'one size fits all' approach to team business. Here are five possible strategies.

1 For those elements of meetings that are to do with conveying information, a group e-mail or an online presentation will often do the trick, and if steps are taken to set up question and feedback options that are visible and accessible to all participants, then questions can be dealt with in a manner that doesn't prove a boring waste of time for more informed members of the group.

2 Where the aim is to elicit views, a proposition can be made under a discussion thread started within an e-mail group. These are online discussion groups in which a topic can be pursued thoroughly with all interested parties having their say. There are numerous packages that can provide this sort of service, and larger organizations will tend to have such facilities available through their intranets and software such as Microsoft SharePoint. However, for those who don't have such facilities, it's a simple matter to set up a private group in a free service such as Google or Yahoo Groups. Your group can be limited to an invited membership, those colleagues with whom you would normally need to meet, and discussion cannot be viewed by anyone who is not a group member.

3 In many circumstances e-mail and instant messaging can be an irritating interruption to other work, but if used properly they can reduce considerably the time that has to be spent in meetings, offering as they do a simple and immediate means of sharing ideas and answering questions.

4 One of the most significant benefits of cloud-based computing, where applications and documents reside on remote servers rather than individual computers, is the facility it offers for individuals to collaborate on projects without ever needing to be in the same place at the same time:

a. documents which are available to a whole group can be revised and worked upon with each individual's contribution being clearly identified;

b. shared access to project software and task lists in the cloud can greatly facilitate communication on group activity – serving to clarify responsibilities, and maintaining an up-to-date record of progress towards objectives.

c. shared notebooks in applications such as Microsoft OneNote, can be a useful way for team members to generate and share ideas, work upon solutions to problems and communicate new information;

Once again, larger organizations are likely to be set up for such collaboration, but anyone using Microsoft Windows 7 or later, or recent Apple devices can access the cloud facilities that come with the operating system. There is also a host of other networked storage services, such as the popular application Dropbox (www.dropbox.com) offering free online storage and shared access where required.

5 Video conferencing offers one major advantage over the traditional meeting – the absence of any requirement for participants to travel – but it does suffer a couple of disadvantages. For those new to the medium, consciousness of being on camera can lead to less natural behaviour than would be the case in a face-to-face encounter. This somewhat artificial atmosphere may be exacerbated by hardware limitations, such as the phenomenon whereby participants appear not to be making eye contact – the result of them being filmed by a camera at a slightly different angle to the screen on which their attention is focused. Studies have also shown that participants in video conferences have to work harder to interpret information than would be the case in a live meeting.

So, in situations where there is no need for face-to-face contact or for visual images to be displayed, an audio conference call may be just as effective as a video conference. However, for many meeting scenarios, video conferencing has a great deal to offer all manner of businesses small and large, and is accessible even on the tightest of budgets. There are numerous packages, providing differing levels of quality over a wide price range, but at the simplest end it is possible, very cheaply, to set up a Skype subscription to handle group video calls for up to ten simultaneous participants using standard webcams.

DELEGATE

Edward Newton reckons to work an average 58-hour week. The company he works for has been going through major changes recently and Edward's job has been closely associated with those changes. He is aware that he tries to do too many things himself and that some tasks could be passed on to other members of his team, but he feels that those he can trust are themselves overloaded. It's also his belief that, in the short term, the time taken to brief and coach somebody else would exceed the time he is currently spending on these tasks. His problem is exacerbated because, in a situation of change, he is unsure how long his workload will remain at the present level, and hence he is reluctant to pass on responsibilities only to take them back later. At the back of his mind there is even a slight worry that he may need his heavy workload to justify his existence in any future restructuring. From time to time he gets so overloaded that he simply has to dump jobs on colleagues with wholly insufficient briefing or assistance.

There are lots of Edwards in every area of work – people whose competence is being stretched to the limit by competition, change and restructuring. They are suffering from the catch-22 situation where they know they ought to delegate more but feel they haven't the time to do it properly. But for anybody who wants to get organized and stay on top of the job, delegation has to be part of the recipe.

The first important point about delegation is that it should not be a knee-jerk reaction to your own overload. It isn't just a matter of offloading tasks you don't want to do, but a contribution to overall productivity by placing responsibility and the necessary authority and resources where they can be discharged most effectively. You will have difficulty with delegation if you're not prepared to invest the time in setting arrangements up, if you can't trust your colleagues or if you cannot believe that anyone else is able to do the job as well as you.

At one time delegation was always seen in terms of tasks being passed to more junior colleagues, but in these days of flatter organizational structures, there is an increased tendency to think of sideways delegation – the movement of work between colleagues at the same or a similar level. This is really more about trading responsibilities than delegating them in the traditional sense. We all have differing skills and work preferences. If a colleague is able to fulfil an area of your responsibility more effectively than you, and you in turn can bring your skills to an aspect of his or her job, then it makes sense to co-operate. However, the fact that the arrangement is between colleagues at the same level should not be a reason for any less care in the setting-up process.

Five steps to effective delegation

1. Decide what you will delegate

The choice of responsibilities to delegate will normally centre on those things that others may do more quickly, more cheaply or more expertly than you, or tasks that can readily be performed within the context of another person's existing job. There will generally be core elements to your own job that you should not consider delegating.

2. Choose the right person

Beware of the natural tendency to load the willing horses or to delegate tasks only to those who have fulfilled similar work in the past. The reasons for delegation are not only about easing your own workload but about giving new development experiences to others.

3. Prepare the ground

You have to be ready to prepare colleagues for what you want them to do. Time to do this is often an issue, but it is a matter of short-term pain for long-term gain. If you don't set the arrangement up properly, you are likely to have disgruntled colleagues feeling they have been dumped on or people unclear about what is expected of them. You will need to set clear objectives using the SMART formula we discussed in Chapter 1. Let your colleague know the parameters of his or her authority and what support you will be able to provide.

4. Sell the benefits

It's important to look at these from the other person's point of view. There may be training and development benefits to him or her in taking on a new responsibility, enhancement of career prospects, variety and challenge, or opportunity to use particular skills. Be prepared to spend time talking to the person concerned, seeking responses to what you are proposing, and responding constructively. If your colleague can feel that the setting-up process is a collaborative one, he or she will be more committed to taking it on.

5. Stand back

Let the other person get on with it. One of the most common delegation problems is a tendency to interfere or reject the work because it is not being done in exactly the way you would have done it. You need to work hard to avoid this, particularly if you have been doing the job yourself for some time. You should make it clear that you are available to offer support, but that day-to-day responsibility is down to the person to whom you have delegated it. If you don't, it will remain essentially your responsibility, for which you have simply contracted out part of the donkey work. When problems occur, they will wind up back on your plate, and your colleague will not achieve the development benefits that delegation can offer. Of course, the authority you delegate is not limitless, and the person taking on the responsibility should be aware of its limits, but he or she also needs the freedom to operate and sometimes to make mistakes and learn from them.

OVERCOMING DISTRACTIONS AND INTERRUPTIONS

Interruptions and distractions impose heavily on our ability to organize work schedules. Not only is there the actual time lost through the interruption but, more importantly, the effort of getting back to the original task and re-focusing attention. The extent to which we are distracted from our work has become much more acute in recent years as a result of technological advances. We live and work in a world where we are constantly connected, often simultaneously, to multiple communication vehicles – e-mail, the web, mobile phone calls, texts and instant messaging – not to mention our face-to-face interactions with people and the impact of old-fashioned landline telecommunication. In many settings, this ever-present connectedness is regarded as an essential aspect of working life, and multitasking has become the order of the day. But multitasking is not something that human beings are terribly good at. We manage it well enough if we're concerned with activities that demand only minimal attention, but we find it very much more difficult when engaged in those requiring creativity, abstract thought or sustained focus.

A study in 2007 conducted by Microsoft Research and the University of Illinois found that it can take up to 15 minutes to productively resume a challenging task when interrupted by something as simple as an e-mail. And interruptions can result in reduced accuracy of memory too. They interfere with the business of processing information between short-term and long-term memory. It has been found that in some occupations workers are having to switch their attention every few minutes, and the detrimental effects of this are becoming so widely acknowledged that a new term – 'continuous partial attention syndrome' – is increasingly used to describe them.

Of course, not all distractions and interruptions are technological in nature. Some are social, often by people who are themselves engaged in procrastination over tasks they want to escape. You may even be the source of the distraction. It is very easy to convince yourself that you just have to make a phone call, get a coffee or check your favourite blog, and you will be back on track in a few minutes. Once the pattern of work is disrupted, you find other pressing chores and the minutes stretch to an hour or more, after which time it is much harder to pick up the threads.

You will never be able to get rid of interruptions entirely, but you can do a lot to reduce them, and to make those remaining as brief and purposeful as possible. Aim to cut out all bar the most urgent and important – those things that impinge on the key purpose of your job or the organization you work for, and where the consequences of failure to give the matter your immediate attention may be of detriment to either.

The great benefit of e-mail, voicemail and text messaging should be their time independence, and you will certainly be far more productive if you are able to deal with them at times of your choosing rather than when they arrive. Research has shown that people handle messages and other interruptions much more effectively if they occur at natural break points in the other activities they are carrying out. If it is possible for you to do so, set two or three times each day when you will routinely check and deal with calls and messages, and be disciplined about sticking to this routine.

Unfortunately for many readers, this may seem like an unachievable luxury. If you work in a culture where there is an expectation of immediate responses to calls and messages, it may feel almost impossible to free yourself of constant interruptions. But if you want to get the important things done, it is essential that you look for ways to balance accessibility and productivity. You might consider an approach that mirrors the triage techniques used in emergency medicine – filtering out those messages which have to be dealt with immediately from the rest that can wait until a more convenient time. If the facility is available, then one way to get a handle on the important issues quickly is to set your e-mail software just to download headers rather than the full message. You reduce the temptation to deal with each message immediately if another action is required before you can read it, and you can usually tell which messages are important from the header information. It's also a good idea to turn off audible notification of incoming messages and texts. There's nothing more likely to make us interrupt what we are doing than the urgent beep of an arriving message.

You may also like to think about giving yourself e-mail free periods during the day – times when you can work uninterrupted on tasks that require your complete attention. You will probably need to let people know why they are not getting an immediate reply by setting up an auto-responder message along the following lines: 'Thanks for your message. I'm busy on a task that requires all my attention, and can't respond immediately. I check my e-mails regularly and will get back to you today.'

If you're concerned about ensuring accessibility for important messages even during your e-mail free periods, you might consider setting your e-mail software to give you an audible or on-screen alert only when messages from particular senders or those containing certain words in the header are received. Some e-mail applications won't have this facility, and with others it will be rendered inoperative if you have chosen to download just headers. An alternative strategy is to designate a second e-mail address for urgent messages and to set this up for immediate notification.

Fifteen more ways to reduce interruptions

1 Be clear about what you are trying to achieve in your day. Following the advice on planning and tracking your time in Chapter 2 will help you to rate the importance of distractions and interruptions, and keep your focus on what matters in terms of overall productivity.

2 Consolidate tasks such as sending messages and making phone calls to avoid each one becoming a separate interruption to your workflow. You will handle them more effectively and save significant amounts of time that may currently be spent re-focusing after each interruption.

3 Return phone calls at times when people are unlikely to be keen to enter lengthy conversations – just before lunch, or at the end of the day when they want to get home. Alternatively, set timed calls when agreeing to phone back – 'I've got five minutes to spare between appointments at four o'clock. Can I phone you then?'

4 Give thorough briefings when passing on tasks to others, so that they have less need to come back to you with follow-up questions.

5 Clarify instructions and address any weaknesses in procedures that lead to repeated queries, and deal with requests quickly to avoid people chasing you.

6 Set regular times each day when you will deal with those tasks that require uninterrupted concentration and will be unavailable for meetings, calls and other interruptions. Stick to it rigidly and, with luck, others will come to respect your interruption-free zone.

7 If you work in an open plan environment and have no other way of signalling times when you don't wish to be interrupted, consider using an 'OK to Disturb/Please Do Not Disturb' card by your desk.

8 Help to foster a climate conducive to effective work by treating colleagues as you would have them treat you. Avoid excessive copying or forwarding of unimportant e-mails to others, and don't expect people to refrain from interrupting you, if you're in the habit of interrupting them.

9 Take breaks at predetermined times. Build them into a constructive work routine, so that they start to work against self-inflicted interruptions.

10 Remember that cluttered workspace is a potent source of visual distraction. Follow the advice in the next chapter to help reduce any tendency to flit from task to task.

11 Consider working from home when you have a task that needs concentrated thought. Provided that your home doesn't have its own distractions, you may be able to achieve more in a few hours of peace than is possible in a busy workplace.

12 Explore a reciprocal arrangement with colleagues whereby you divert your phone to others so that they can take messages when you need to work on a task interrupted, and you do the same for them at other times.

13 When carrying out work on the internet, beware of following hyperlinks that lead you to other interesting but irrelevant material.

14 If you have senior colleagues who consider that every summons constitutes a reason for you to drop everything, be prepared to work patiently and diplomatically with them to improve awareness of the effects of their behaviour. Share with them, at times other than when they are interrupting you, the measures you are taking to manage your day, and demonstrate the effectiveness of your strategy by your results.

15 Free yourself from the belief that you have to be constantly connected if you want to work effectively. While there are many benefits to today's instant communication culture, there are equally considerable disadvantages. As noted earlier, effective

multitasking is largely a myth. Only by switching off or otherwise limiting sources of interruption for at least part of your working day, will you be able to present yourself with the space to carry out tasks requiring concentrated attention.

Keeping interruptions brief and productive

When interruptions are unavoidable, aim to make them as short as possible. Here are some ideas:

1 Put a time limit on the interruption. Let the person interrupting you know that you can only spare, say, five minutes. Some experts suggest keeping an egg timer on your desk and using it to remind your visitor to get to the point quickly.

2 Risk being considered rude by not inviting interrupters to sit down.

3 Position office furniture and desk to avoid giving your working area a 'please walk in and sit down' appearance. This is particularly important if you are in an open-plan office.

4 Encourage colleagues to come with a bullet point note of what they want to talk to you about. This helps you to tune into the issue quickly, helps them to focus their thinking, and deters more frivolous interruptions because of the preparation involved.

5 If you have difficulty drawing interruptions to a conclusion and sending visitors on their way, think about your body language and the verbal cues within a conversation that allow you to wrap the meeting up without unduly offending the other person.

HELP OTHERS TO BE MORE ORGANIZED

In spite of all your attempts to organize your own schedule and way of working, the disorganization of others can still throw you into confusion, so it's worth giving some attention to strategies for greater organization among those around you.

Disorganized colleagues

Lecturing people on their lack of organization will seldom lead to much more than grudging compliance and, as none of us are wholly without fault, it will often be accompanied by privately exchanged grumbles of, 'He/she's a fine one to talk'. Getting people to articulate their own difficulties and the tactics they can adopt to resolve them is likely to be far more productive. This is generally a matter of asking the right questions in a setting which encourages reflection – a one-to-one meeting or appraisal, for example. Help your colleagues to focus on one thing at a time, and give immediate positive reinforcement in the form of praise and encouragement when you see them working to change their ways. Reinforcement is a very powerful motivator for change, so don't wait until the altered behaviour hits you between the eyes. Actively look for things to praise. Peer pressure can also be a strong influence on individual behaviour. It may be worth considering whether there is mileage in a whole-team initiative aimed at working towards improved effectiveness.

Disorganized boss

A disorganized boss can be a nightmare to work for, but don't treat his or her weaknesses simply as gripes to be shared with other colleagues over coffee. Provided you go about it the right way, you can make a difference, but you will need to be content to work on those aspects of your boss's behaviour that you can influence, and put up with those you can't. Make sure that your own work and organization cannot be faulted, and avoid full-frontal challenges unless you have another job to go to. Here are five traits frequently displayed by disorganized bosses with suggestions on what to do about them.

Inability to make a decision

Remember that bosses are seldom masters of their own destiny. Rather than fuming over what might seem at first sight to be indecisiveness and negativity, make an attempt to understand the politics in which they are operating, and give them the ammunition to fight battles further up the line. Recognize also that your boss may have difficulty tuning in to an issue which has been the focus of your attention for days or even weeks. Be prepared to talk through the thought processes which have led to the conclusions you have reached.

A tendency towards snap decisions

This species lies at the other end of the scale from the indecisive boss and will deal with any question by delivering top-of-the-head certainties. Anything that smacks of thinking time or consideration of alternatives is for wimps. Never approach such a boss with an open-ended question unless you want to find yourself saddled with unworkable solutions and impossible deadlines. Work out the options beforehand and present them with a cogently argued thumbnail guide. The boss will normally want to be credited with a decision, so build in at least one point where there is a choice to be made between alternatives, neither of which would be disastrous.

Inability to end meetings

If your boss is the sort of person who finds it difficult to conclude a meeting, make sure that you have another pressing engagement which allows you an escape route within a reasonable time.

Failure to set clear objectives or focus on the important issues

Clarify your aims and objectives by writing down what you think they are and getting your boss to confirm them. In one-to-one meetings with your boss, provide a written summary of the issues for discussion and list possible solutions to problems.

Inability to remember what he or she has asked you to do

Develop a practice of taking notes whenever you meet to discuss tasks, and sending your boss an action note detailing what you have agreed to do, as soon as possible afterwards.

LEARN TO SAY 'NO'

A large part of organizing yourself is about remaining in control of your workload. If you always say 'yes' to requests that come your way, then you lose that control. You over-burden yourself, with the resultant stress, and by saying 'yes' to unimportant requests you may find yourself unable to fulfil key objectives. There are a number of reasons why saying 'no' may be difficult:

- You don't want to appear unwilling and spoil your prospects.
- You're concerned that you might displease others or hurt their feelings.
- You underestimate the increased pressure you will be under as a result of saying 'yes'.
- You simply don't realize that saying 'no' is an option.

Of course, you don't want to get a reputation for negativity – a knee-jerk 'no' may be worse than a knee-jerk 'yes'. If you are in the process of establishing yourself in a new job or interest group, you may need to say 'yes' more often than is good for you. But it is important to be able to draw the line skilfully and assertively, and recognize that it is impossible to please everyone all the time. Decide which requests you need to turn down by asking yourself:

- How does this fit with my main objectives?
- Will my prospects be affected if I don't do it?
- What else might I need to drop or postpone in order to undertake this? What will be the effect of that on other objectives?

- Will doing it result in any detrimental lifestyle effect – significantly increased stress, unreasonable intrusion on my leisure time?
- Will I miss out on any opportunity to develop a new skill if I don't do this?

Try a balance sheet approach – pluses on one side, minuses on the other – where the choice is difficult.

How to do it

There are three ways of approaching 'no'.

Aggressive approach

Complains loudly about being overburdened and taken for granted. Accuses the person making the request of being unreasonable, rants or bursts into tears.

Timid approach

Responds to the request with mumbled attempts to delay a decision. Leaves the person making the request unclear about whether 'yes' or 'no' has been said. Wastes energy fretting about the request and ends up doing it resentfully.

Assertive approach

Indicates pleasure at being asked, but explains succinctly and politely why he or she is unable to respond positively. Suggests possible alternative ways of getting the task done, and specifies what support he or she can offer to whoever takes on the task.

Needless to say, the third is the approach you should aim for. The person making the request is under no misapprehension about your response or the reasons for it, but does not come away from the encounter angry and brow-beaten; and you do not damage your reputation for helpfulness and positive thinking.

When faced with an unexpected request or put on the spot for an immediate response, it can be difficult instantly to weigh up the pros and cons of the proposition, and there may be an inclination to answer yes to something you might later regret. In such circumstances ask for time to consider the request, and give your reasons, for example the need to take account of its impact on your overall workload. If you're dealing with a reasonable person, they will hopefully recognize the validity of your response and agree to a deferred response.

Take particular care with requests where the commitment asked of you is not immediate, but comes at some time in the future – a request to make a presentation at a conference, for example. When the event is three months away, it's easy to be over-optimistic about the time you will have to fit in the necessary preparation. But as the day approaches and you find your schedule ever more crowded, the additional task assumes the status of an unwelcome addition to a heavy workload, and you end up resentfully turning out a rush job which doesn't do you justice. Awareness of priorities, clarity about your schedule and control over planning are the ways to ensure that you don't fall into this trap.

SUMMARY

You can achieve greater effectiveness in those aspects of your work that involve others by:

- helping to ensure that the meetings you attend are as productive as possible;
- delegating in the right way and for the right reasons;
- actively working to beat distractions and interruptions;
- recognizing that you can help others to be more organized;
- learning to say no assertively.

ORGANIZE YOUR SPACE

The way you organize your space can have a considerable effect on your productivity – saving time, preventing fatigue, allowing you to complete tasks more quickly. But it's very easy to become accustomed to a working environment that is less than ideal, so take a few minutes to look at your office with a fresh eye:

- How often do you have to get up from your chair to retrieve things that are out of reach?
- Is there space and absence of clutter on your desktop to allow you to work comfortably and without distraction?
- Are your computer keyboard and monitor positioned so that you can use them comfortably and without undue fatigue?
- Is there space adjacent to your computer workstation for any papers you need while you are working at it?
- Are your cupboards, drawers and bookcases crammed with items you don't need?
- Is your storage equipment appropriate for the items you need to keep in it?

- Do you regularly have to spend time searching for things?
- Is your office furniture best positioned for your different needs – working at your desk, using the computer, meeting with colleagues or customers?

There is no standard recipe for organizing your work space – what feels comfortable to you may not to somebody else – but there are some general principles that you should consider in arriving at the best arrangement for you.

THINK ABOUT ERGONOMICS

Ergonomics is the process of designing machines, work methods and environments to take into account the safety, comfort and productivity of human users. It might sound rather grand when applied to the business of organizing your work space, but there is no doubt that the choice and positioning of furniture, equipment, reference material and accessories can have a major impact on the way you work.

Furniture

Desks

Your desk needs sufficient clear space for you to be able to work comfortably and without distraction. We will come onto clearing the clutter a little later. If you have to divide your time between computer and paperwork, consider a modern wrap-around style which allows you to move between a traditional desktop and computer workstation without getting up. If you have any choice in the matter, go for a desk with adjustable height settings. Consider how the desk is placed in relation to your office space as a whole. Positioning your desk so that it forms a barrier between you and any visitor creates psychological distance. This may be the effect you want to create, but think about moving it if you want to give a more accessible impression. A desk which faces a wall may offer access to handy space for shelves, pinboards, etc. For those working in an open-plan office, facing a wall or screen serves to minimize distractions and casual interruptions.

Chairs

Most modern office chairs are designed with castors and swivel action, allowing you to move easily to different parts of your workstation, and providing good back support to prevent fatigue. Reject those which are a triumph of ostentation over ergonomics, and signal more about your position in the organization than your productivity.

There is no such thing as an ideal chair for everybody, but there are certain features you should look for:

- adjustable seat height;
- a backrest which is adjustable both vertically and in a forward–backward direction;
- seat depth which is sufficient if you are tall but not too great if you are short;
- adequate stability;
- castors, if required, which are appropriate for the type of flooring in your office.

Other equipment

It is a good idea to review from time to time the locations of those accessories and items of equipment you use regularly. They should be immediately to hand when you need them. If you have shelves above your desk, it should be possible to reach the items on the lowest one without standing up. Avoid placing items you use frequently – telephone, printer, reference books – in positions where you will need to stretch or twist in order to use them. Have an eye to the changing nature of your job. It's quite often the case that we leave reference books or items of equipment in easily accessible places long after they have ceased to be vital parts of our daily routine, while other things that have assumed greater importance are left out of reach. As little as 20 minutes spent reorganizing your immediate workspace can pay productivity dividends.

Lighting

Many of the lighting problems in modern offices are associated with computer use, but it is important to have the right sort of lighting conditions for other activities too. Diffusers on overhead lights and the use of desk lamps can help to provide more comfortable conditions for reading and working with printed material.

Use of the computer

If your activities involve sustained computer use, taking some simple steps can enhance your productivity, increase your comfort and protect against injury and fatigue.

Here is a ten point checklist to follow:

1 Position monitors so that light is not reflected off them, and take care that you're not dealing with extremes of contrast. A monitor placed in front of a window, where sunlight on the outside contrasts sharply with the screen, can be very hard on the eyes. Use window blinds and diffusers on overhead lighting to counteract these problems.

2 To prevent neck strain, ensure that the top of your monitor screen is no higher than eye level.

3 Sit with a comfortable and balanced posture, and keep your forearms, wrists and hands in a straight line. Your keyboard should be at the same angle as the forearms.

4 Don't rest your forearms or wrists on sharp edges, and don't hit the keyboard too hard.

5 Take frequent breaks from sustained computer activity. Experts suggest 5 to 10 minutes every hour.

6 Rest your eyes every 10 or 15 minutes by closing them momentarily, gazing at a distant object and blinking frequently.

7 Clean computer screens regularly.

8 Don't get too close to the screen. It may strain both your eyes and neck. This tendency is often the result of wearing standard reading glasses for computer work. You may need glasses with an intermediate prescription that allows you to focus at the right distance.

9 Reading paper documents generally requires better illumination than reading from computer screens. If you are working with paper and computer simultaneously, an adjustable desk light is useful to provide additional light on the paper without casting a glare on the screen.

10 A copy holder will make it easier for you to view any documents you are using while working on the computer. If you are able to keep your paper copy at roughly the same distance from your eyes as the monitor screen, it saves you having to refocus every time you look from one to the other.

Extra considerations for portable computer use

The power and capacity of laptop computers have increased markedly in recent years, to the point that many people now use them in place of desktop computers. This can lead to ergonomic difficulties that may have a significant impact on health. Problems arise primarily from the compact nature of portable computers. Keyboards tend to be smaller, the keys closer together and intensive use of them can increase the risk of repetitive strain injury. Screen sizes are generally smaller than those for desktop computers which may lead to greater eyestrain, and pointing devices such as touchpads may not be as ergonomically advantageous as the traditional mouse. The biggest problems, however, are those affecting the posture of the user, and arise from the fact that screen and keyboard are part of the same unit and as such are too close together for best usability. Essentially, if the keyboard is in the best position for typing the screen is too low, leading to a typical laptop crouch that can create neck and back problems, whereas if the screen is in the best position for viewing, the user's hands at the keyboard are too high. While this is not a problem for limited use, it starts to create difficulties when the laptop is used extensively.

The best advice for those using a laptop as their main machine is to set up a docking station arrangement whereby they are able to connect a standard monitor, keyboard and mouse. A cheaper alternative is to buy just a keyboard and mouse and to elevate the screen using a laptop stand. For those who use a laptop actually in their lap, not something to be done for lengthy periods of time, it's important to raise the rear of the machine to get the best available angle for viewing and typing. You can do this with a wedge shaped laptop pad, or by putting your feet on a stool to raise the knees.

There is not as yet much research on the health implications of extensive computer tablet use, but a study by the Harvard School of Public Health has suggested that they can place considerable strain on users' neck muscles, as a result of hunching when typing. Once again, the use of a separate keyboard is advised and increasingly there are stands and docking stations that allow the screen to be placed at a better angle to the user.

TACKLE DISORGANIZED WORK SPACE

Disorganized work space is a potent source of wasted time and unnecessary stress. Tackling it is a tangible commitment to a more effective way of working. The area on and around your desk is the most important part of your working environment, and you might be tempted to tackle it first. But I suggest that you begin by clearing cupboards and drawers, in order to free up space to accommodate items that are cluttering your immediate desk area.

Organizing cupboards, drawers and bookcases

These are all handy hiding places for things you don't need. Start by looking at the cupboards furthest away from your desk – they are likely to have the greatest proportion of redundant material, untouched by previous purges – and move inwards towards your desk. That way you will always have space to house items that are currently jamming up more immediate working areas. Clear out the junk ruthlessly. If there are items that really cannot be discarded, but hardly ever need to be looked at, put them in archive boxes or another long-term storage facility. Remember to take a note of the box contents and file it where you will be able to find it.

Work through all your cupboards and drawers, discarding junk, grouping like items together and making sure that items such as box files are clearly labelled. With bookcases it helps to take everything out before rearranging according to subject matter. The fact that books come in stubbornly different sizes means that you won't be able to achieve perfect organization, and you shouldn't waste time trying. All you are attempting to do is organize material so that you can quickly put your hand on it when the need arises.

Organizing your desk space

For all the explosion of electronic communication in recent years, many of us still have to deal with large quantities of printed material in our working lives. I used to pretend that I could work well with a cluttered desk. Despite the various piles of paper, at times threatening to engulf the workspace, I claimed that I could easily put my hand on any document I needed and that shifting my attention from one task to another kept me sharp throughout my working day. It was nonsense, of course. Superfluous papers are a distraction from the job in hand in much the same way as interruptions and phone calls. It is all too easy to flit around a crowded desk, pecking at tasks rather than devoting the concentrated effort needed to complete them. The presence of a multiplicity of documents is also an excuse for procrastination. When you are struggling with one task, it's the simplest thing in the world to shift your energy and attention to another, seemingly more straightforward chore which beckons from the top of a nearby pile.

Searching can waste considerable amounts of time and throw up further distractions. Just consider the number of times you need to root through the piles when a request or phone call summons the presence of a particular piece of paper. Surveys have suggested that 15 minutes a day is a fairly conservative estimate. It doesn't sound much, does it? But when you consider that 15 minutes a day is equal to a week and a half out of every year, the waste of your time is much more apparent. What could you do with that time? If you are disorganized to the extent that you spend 30 minutes a day searching for things, then the reward for greater discipline could be almost three weeks of additional productive activity.

Desktop disorganization also destroys your ability to set priorities. Within the same pile there may be scribbled notes, half-drafted reports, important letters and complete junk. All share a common fate – their importance is only considered when they come to the top of the pile or force themselves on your consciousness in the course of a search for something else.

And then there is the sheer inefficiency of it all. When you start a new task you have to clear some working space, pushing previously incomplete activity into yet higher piles. The same items pass through your hands numerous times, surfacing and resurfacing from the confusion of papers. You waste energy on things that should have been discarded the very first time you saw them. You miss deadlines because the papers that would remind you of them are buried under heaps of other stuff. You even find yourself sorting through the waste paper basket for that important piece of information you remember scribbling on a scrap of paper, which might have been the one which made no sense to you when you picked it out of the pile this morning.

Finally there is the stress. All the time that your untackled paperwork is an amorphous mass, it represents a potent source of disquiet. You are not entirely sure what lurks within those piles and they remain an ever-present reminder of your failure to get on top of your job. Very often the awareness of tasks to be done is more stressful than actually doing them.

So are you convinced? Sure. All that remains now is to do something about it. Simplicity has to be the keynote of your desk organization. One of everything is a good place to start – one in tray, one out tray, one diary, one notebook. Think about whether you need personal clutter around your desktop. You may want to keep the odd photo or memento but there should be no sense in which personal reminders impose on your ability to work effectively. Accessories and equipment on your desktop should consist of items that you use daily. Other things may be kept close to hand but away from your main working surface. Give yourself plenty of space to work. There is a psychological advantage to the absence of clutter as well as a physical one.

You may need to overcome a mental hurdle in clearing your desk. There is a tendency to associate the crowded desk with a busy owner, and we like to think of ourselves as busy. Remember, however, that one can be busy but incompetent and unproductive. Let the results of your activities speak for you rather than the appearance of your desk. Once you are clear about what has a place on your desk, you are ready to tackle the piles.

ELIMINATE PAPER PILES

The prospect of tackling the piles of paper which have built up on your desk and around your office may be intimidating, but by setting aside some time for a disciplined blitz, you can get rid of them and lift the mental weight of their presence. In addition to items which need action on your part or should be directed to others, it is likely that your paper piles will consist of documents (reports, periodicals, etc) which you have put aside to be read later, items which have not made it to the filing cabinet, and things which you were not sure what to do with.

Your objective is to get through the paper piles; you must not let yourself become bogged down. So, be prepared to attack the offending heaps and deal quickly and decisively with their contents (Figure 6.1):

Figure 6.1 Eliminate the paper piles

- **Earmark four empty folders, filing trays or baskets and mark them: Deal with, Distribute, Read, File.**
  Make sure you have sufficient sturdy plastic bin bags for the most important category – the discard pile.
- **Approach the task with the view that the majority of items are destined for the bin.**
  Whatever relevance they had when they joined the pile is likely to have diminished. Don't repeat previous indecisiveness. If in doubt, throw it out.
- **Don't waste time reading items.**
  Skim them to the point of determining whether they are needed and if so put them in the relevant tray or basket.
- **Don't file or act upon things as you go; you will become bogged down and distracted.**

By all means mark items to assist your actions and filing later, but keep to your main objective – to blast through the pile.

- **Zip through magazines and periodicals.**
  Tear out the pages containing articles you wish to keep and throw the rest away. Don't stop to read any of them at this stage.

- **When you have worked your way through the piles, turn your attention to the four trays.**
  Schedule time to deal with the reading and filing tasks, and use a 'bring forward' system with a concertina file or reminders in your PIM to determine when the 'deal with' items will be actioned.

Tackled in this way, a fearsome chore can become a real stress buster.

Keeping your work space organized

OK, so you've managed to sort the contents of your office. The things you use regularly are close at hand, you have ditched the junk and cleared the piles. How do you keep it that way?

The answer is, I'm afraid, a boring one. It has a lot to do with developing positive work habits:

- Move paperwork quickly in line with the five Ds outlined in Chapter 4.

- If in doubt throw it out!

- Don't use your desk as filing space – use project folders or 'bring forward' files for work in progress.

- Keep your equipment needs under review. Are the items you use regularly still in the most accessible places?

- Don't transfer piles of paper on your desk to piles of paper in other parts of the office.

- Try to file on a daily basis. When you remove items from your filing cabinets, make a practice of re-filing them as soon as possible.

CLEAR CLUTTER AT HOME

Everything that has been written about organizing your work-space applies just as much to your home. If you're living amid clutter it will affect your ability to do the things you want to do, both in work and leisure terms. And a cluttered home is even more common than a cluttered workspace – we have a psychological attachment to many of the things that we bring into our homes and can display a surprising degree of reluctance to discard items that have long since outlived their usefulness. What's more, around the home there tend to be lots more places where clutter can accumulate.

Clutter isn't just unsightly, it's a potent source of wasted time. The list of things we spend time looking for around the home can be quite lengthy: tools, utensils, stationery items, keys, books and magazines, clothes and shoes, letters, bills and receipts, DVDs and CDs, directories and address books. You may even think of some additional categories that apply in your own case. Take a moment to ask yourself what are the main items you spend time looking for and what are the reasons you regularly misplace them. Could it be because they don't have habitual storage locations to which they are routinely replaced? Or is it because the items concerned are simply overwhelmed among lots of other clutter that should have been discarded? You might like to conduct an audit of your own situation over a period of days as a way of galvanizing yourself into action.

So, how do you bring some organization into your home space to accompany the steps you have taken in your work area?

You can start with a similar sort of blitz to the one I described earlier in relation to office workspace, but don't try to tackle the whole house at once. Take it a room at a time. Once again separate items into four categories, but this time make them: items to keep, items to store, items to donate to the charity shop and items to ditch. Be particularly ruthless with the 'items to store' category. Rather like paperwork filing, you can be pretty sure that most of the things you pile into the loft will never be needed again.

Once you have decided what you are going to keep, make sure there is a suitable home for everything. Magazines that go back into a pile will start the clutter cycle all over again. Work hard over the next three or four weeks at returning items to their proper place until you have built up a regular habit. While you're achieving this, it's a good idea to have a mini purge at the end of each day, putting things away. Just as with your workspace, take care to house the things you use frequently in the most accessible locations.

Ensure that you have suitable storage for the things you are going to keep. A filing system that you habitually maintain for essential paperwork is often just as much a priority in the home as it is in the office. Stackable storage boxes can be useful for those objects that aren't readily housed in drawers or cupboards. Just make sure that you label them appropriately and keep like items together, so that you don't have to rummage through the lot whenever you want a single item.

In working to build up an organized habit, pay particular attention to the places where things tend to accumulate – the kitchen table, for example, or by the front door. Make a rule that for every new item of furniture or equipment you acquire, you will get rid of something. With items that you have in multiple numbers, ask yourself seriously how many you really need, and get rid of those surplus to requirements.

SUMMARY

The key aspects of organizing your space are:

- arranging your furniture and equipment to maximize safety, comfort and productivity;
- freeing up time and space by reorganizing your desk and storage space;
- reducing stress by eliminating stacks of paper around your office;
- tackling the clutter around your home.

ORGANIZE FILING SYSTEMS

Not many years ago, a chapter such as this would have been all about the physical storage of documents. Today, we need to take account of the sheer amount of information that never finds its way into print – e-mails, web pages, shared electronic files – as well as the options for electronic storage of paper documents, and we will do so later in the chapter.

Nevertheless, it's with traditional manual storage that we will start. Regardless of how technically geared up you are, it is likely that there will continue to be documents you will keep in paper form. Original hard copy may be required for legal or taxation reasons, or it may be simply that some items would be too much of a hassle to store electronically.

Surveys have consistently shown that filing is the organizational chore that people hate the most, and our very loathing of it may mean that we give insufficient attention to doing it well. The only reason for putting a document into a file is so that you can find it again, and the only reason you might want to do that is to help you fulfil some aspect of your future work.

Up to 85 per cent of the material stored in the average filing cabinet is never referred to again. That means, for every five documents painstakingly categorized, punched and filed, possibly just one will be needed in the future. And the chances are that the one that is needed will prove frustratingly difficult to locate. It's a case of the 85 per cent you don't need getting in the way of the 15 per cent that you do.

You can never predict with certainty those documents you will need again. Some things do need to be stored on a 'just in case' basis, but you can drastically cut down on the chore of filing and failure to find the documents you need by more confident use of the 'discard' option when you first receive material. Filing is not a matter of getting a document off your desk when you're frightened to throw it away, but are not sure what else to do with it. A document should only make it to the filing cabinet when it cannot be readily accessed elsewhere and there is a reasonable chance that it will be needed again in the future.

If you can step away from a defensive filing mentality – better save it, just in case – to an attacking frame of mind, then you have much more chance of getting yourself a lean, mean filing system that works for you. For every document you consider filing, ask yourself 'What use will this document be to me in the future?' If you don't get a convincing answer, ditch it.

In addition to defensive filing, there are a number of other common document storage problems. How many of the following apply to you:

- inappropriately located information?
- no structure to the filing system?
- a structure which hasn't been kept to?
- insufficient thought given to the appropriate grouping of items to allow for easy retrieval?
- failure to weed out obsolete material?

- forgetting what files you already have and setting up folders which duplicate existing categories of information?

- filing material that is easily accessible elsewhere?

- setting up too many categories within a system so that it becomes unmanageable?

- use of inappropriate storage equipment for particular types of material (eg suspended files straining to hold weighty reports and periodicals)?

- time spent searching for things which have been misfiled?

- indecision about where to put things?

- missing files that have been 'borrowed' by a person or persons unknown?

Locate information appropriately

Your choice of location and storage medium should take account of the frequency with which you may need to consult files.

Current projects and activities

These are files which you may need to consult several times in the course of a day and so should be kept either in desk filing drawers or in a filing cart immediately next to your desk. As well as files for individual projects or assignments in progress, you may want to earmark a file each for correspondence pending, reading and meetings. They can help you to avoid the tendency to put things back into your in tray or to create piles on your desk. If you choose this approach, you need to take care that these files don't become general dumping areas. 'To read' files are particularly prone to this. General files may also result in date-related information being overlooked – preparatory reading for a meeting, for example, or a letter which needs to be answered by a particular date. Use a concertina file with a 'bring forward' system to overcome this problem.

Main reference files

Your main filing system is for the things you need to refer to from time to time. Material from the current projects and activities category will find its way there provided it is worth keeping. Don't simply transfer current project files to your main filing cabinet when the project is completed. Very often they will be cluttered with working papers and rough drafts that are of no further significance. Ruthlessly weed out the junk if you want to be able to lay your hands on the important stuff.

SETTING UP YOUR FILING SYSTEM

First decide on broad divisions in which you want to group your files. These will clearly depend on the nature of your work, but examples of category titles might include: clients, staff, projects and administration. You might like to consider colour coding files within each category, so that when seeking a file you can quickly go to the right part of the cabinet. This is particularly useful when you are using a lateral filing system rather than a drawer filing cabinet. Alphabetical order is normally the most convenient arrangement for individual files within a category.

In deciding the titles for individual files, choose the broadest possible description consistent with manageability. You will want to avoid the need to split overlarge files within a short time and, equally, will not want to find yourself with lots of files each containing just a few documents. Neither is conducive to easy retrieval, which is the sole reason you are engaged in the task. If your file headings are too broad, then you might as well leave the documents in piles. Don't try to predict all the files you may need in the future – you'll end up with some empty folders if you do – but remember that your system needs the capacity to expand rationally, so allow space within files and sections for it to do so. Keep titles short and simple, and try to avoid descriptions that are vague or woolly. Miscellaneous files are notorious black holes.

Choose storage which is appropriate for the material. Use magazine files or box files rather than hanging folders for bulky reports and periodicals. Consider whether you need to store complete copies of magazines and periodicals. Cuttings take up far less room and it is much easier to find the item you want.

FILING DOCUMENTS

If you are following the paper handling procedures recommended in Chapter 4, you will already have weeded out that which isn't worth keeping. Here are some additional pointers to ensure that your paper storage is as effectively managed as possible:

1 Make a note indicating the intended destination file at the top of any document you have decided to file. This prevents you having to reread and decide on destination when you actually come to file the document.

2 If you are uncertain about where to put an item, think about the most likely context in which you are liable to require it in the future.

3 Keep a list of your files handy to help refresh your memory when deciding where to file an item, and to avoid opening new files which overlap with those that already exist.

4 Don't file hard copy of information already stored on computer. Ensure a sensible directory structure for your computer files with reliable back-up. It is quicker to do, easier to find and amend, and takes up less room.

5 Don't file material which is readily available from other sources such as the originator of the document, central archives, internet reference sources.

6 Build up a filing habit. Spending a little time regularly is much less of a chore than trying to wade through a large pile of documents for filing. Try to file daily if possible.

7 If you are tempted to file an item you haven't been bothered to read, ask yourself a very serious 'Why?'

8 If missing files are a problem in your office, a simple tracking system can be introduced. Keep some A4 cards by the filing cabinets, each divided into three columns: Name, Location, Date. Anybody borrowing a file enters their details on the card and places it in the appropriate empty file pocket.

Pruning and weeding your files

Without regular attention, files can rapidly get out of hand. The storage life of material varies hugely according to the nature of the information. Some items become redundant in a matter of weeks, while others need to be kept for years. Weeding out what needs to be discarded or archived can be daunting. If you are working with a file and notice that it contains obsolete information, weed it out there and then, but don't let yourself be distracted from your current task into a lengthy sorting process.

Try to schedule a regular file overhaul. You may opt either for 'big bang' or for 'little and often'. The former is a trawl through all your files, say, every three months. The latter might mean spending five or ten minutes sorting a couple of files at the end of each day. Both have drawbacks. If you're overloaded, and who isn't these days, the big bang tends to get postponed indefinitely until a very serious problem builds up. Little and often requires some attention to building up a habit.

However you set about the task, you need to be ruthless with the rubbish and not to allow yourself to become bogged down in spin-off tasks. If there are items which have been misplaced, or one file needs to be merged with another, just put the items where they need to go, and resist the temptation to sort the destination file unless it is one you have already dealt with. Its turn will come in due course.

ELECTRONIC FILING OF PAPER DOCUMENTS

Storing documents electronically has the advantage of saving much of the time and space occupied by traditional filing methods, as well as greatly facilitating the sharing of data and retrieval of information. The ever-increasing capacity and tumbling cost of the required hardware mean that an electronic filing system is within the scope of any computer user. All that is needed is a scanner, appropriate software and suitable storage and backup facilities. If you are going to be processing a large number of documents, it helps for the scanner to have an automatic sheet feeder. The necessary software to scan and save your documents will generally come bundled with the scanner, but a relatively inexpensive upgrade or purchase of a leading OCR package such as OmniPage will generally add much greater sophistication and ease of use. Such software will allow you to save your scanned documents in any of the major formats including PDF files which, with their compact size, faithful reproduction of text and graphics, and ability to be made searchable, have become the worldwide standard for shared documents.

Making the switch

You shouldn't expect to make a wholesale switch to digital files casually or immediately. It will take time and planning, and in the initial stages may actually mean more work rather than less. Even with automatic document feeders, scanning remains a chore and not every item comes conveniently in loose sheets. In addition to the items you will always need to retain as paper originals, there may be documents such as bulky bound reports that are simply too much of a hassle to digitize in their entirety. It's inevitable then that for the foreseeable future you will have a dual system, but increasingly those items stored as paper will become the minority. The benefits will start to be seen in terms of less time looking for things, less use of paper, and less space taken up by storage.

For even a small organization it makes sense to plan and phase the switch to digital filing, working from a clear start date when documents of a certain type will be filed this way (for example incoming invoices) and then at a later stage moving on to other forms of documentation. Remember too that there are increasing numbers of documents that will not need scanning because they already arrive in electronic form. Reports, invoices and periodicals that come this way can be filed alongside those you have scanned.

If your aim is to digitize the majority of existing files, then you need to take account of the scale of such an operation. It is probably best carried out gradually in conjunction with your regular file review.

Managing your scanned documents

Once digitized, documents can be treated like any other computer files that you have created and stored in your documents library. However, you may want to consider an application specifically designed to assist you in managing and retrieving electronically filed documents. One such is PaperPort (www.nuance.com). It provides powerful search and retrieval facilities in addition to sophisticated assistance with the process of scanning, conversion into searchable PDF files, annotation where required and organization into easily manageable folders. It also includes the facility to connect to online cloud services such as its own 'PaperPort Anywhere' or others like Windows SkyDrive. Storing your documents in the cloud allows you to access them from any of your portable devices – laptop, phone, tablet – or even to share them with others.

Storage of documents in electronic form rather than on paper puts greater emphasis on reliable backup procedures. Establish automatic, timed backup to ensure that you are not left with a calamitous gap in your records in the event of a serious computer crash.

ORGANIZING COMPUTER FILES

You might feel that, with all the sophisticated file management and search tools now available, attention to organizing your computer files is unnecessary. Desktop search tools are a world away from what they were just a few years ago and finding documents on your computer has never been easier. For users of Windows 7 and beyond, the entry of a single word or phrase in the search box of the Start Menu is sufficient to throw up an instant list of all the files containing that term. Nevertheless, I would still strongly advocate a simple and logical grouping of material into folders and sub-folders. It takes very little time to do, it makes tasks like archiving more straightforward, and there will be occasions when it is easier to go to a sub-folder where you know you can locate a file than to attempt recall of a name or keyword in order to run a search. Furthermore, if you're creating a lot of files with similar content, then desktop search may not be a great deal of help to you.

Needless to say, you should start by ensuring that the files you have created are separate from any program files on your computer. Using the 'Documents' facility (My Documents in Windows XP) provided by your operating system makes it easier to locate them, to back them up and to prevent accidental erasure.

I suggest that you then decide what will be your top level document storage directory. It wouldn't be helpful for me to be too prescriptive on this as the best arrangement will depend on the nature and volume of your work. My preferred approach is to create a new main folder each year for common document types (word processor, spread sheet, presentation, etc) as this allows for easy archiving and prevents subdirectories of routine documents getting out of hand. However, the nature of my work is such that I create a limited number of quite large documents and, for those with a high volume of files, a different balance between current and archive folders is likely to be in order. Many prefer to make groupings such as 'customers' 'suppliers' 'projects' the top level destinations and to shift files related to completed work regularly to similarly named archive folders. Whatever your choice, you will want within your main directories to set up subfolders that provide homes for the different categories of activity and types of routine document you create.

Once you have arrived at the most logical grouping of documents to meet your needs, it's important to stick to the system. If you find yourself with an overly large number of subfolders within a folder, you may need to consider splitting it or indexing the subfolders in some way.

The business of choosing filenames is all about simplicity and accessibility once again. It greatly helps to have filenames that mean something to you when you seek them out. You don't want the irritation and wasted time of opening a file only to find that it is not what you thought it was. If your software automatically offers a filename based on the headings used for the document, this may sometimes be adequate, but frequently such names are overly lengthy and you should take care if you're producing a number of documents that have similar headings. Documents such as letters or minutes may be best saved with a name and date (the yyyy/mm/dd format ensures that they will be arranged in date order – eg Bloggslet20131215 or Safetymtg20130326) so that other documents relating to the same person or meeting can be easily identified. Of course, where you are likely to create a large number of documents related to the same subject, organization or individual, it makes sense to group them within a sub folder. For projects, it is generally helpful to have files of all types – word processing, presentations, spread sheets – within the same folder.

Don't try to save everything. Computer files are a great deal easier to store and retrieve than paper ones, but unnecessary saving can result in jumbled folders with consequent difficulty in finding the items you want. It usually makes sense to get rid of rough drafts and working documents that you have stored on the way to producing major pieces of work, and keep just the final version. However, if there is a good reason for keeping some working documents, make sure that they are clearly identified as such.

Delete unnecessary e-mails and keep only those that require further actions or contain information you may need in the future. Create folders for the e-mails you are going to keep and make a habit of routinely filing them rather than leaving them jamming up your inbox. Set up archiving arrangements so that current folders are cleared of old messages at regular intervals.

SECURING YOUR INFORMATION

Failure to organize the security of your information adequately may leave you with a loss of precious data, time-consuming recovery tasks and embarrassment or worse as far as your employers or clients are concerned. As with most other organizational issues, it's a matter of deciding on your objectives, putting measures in place to achieve them, and building regular habits in order to maintain them.

The security issues most likely to concern you are:

- backup of computer data;
- selection and maintenance of passwords;
- protection from malicious attack;
- physical security of equipment and data;
- security of paper-based information.

Backup

Few office experiences can be more stressful than the complete loss of days, weeks or months of work through inadequate attention to backup. Seldom is it wholly impossible to recover lost information but, depending on the nature of the data loss, recovery may be time-consuming or expensive.

What do you back up?

There are two approaches to backup. You can choose to create a system image (a complete copy of your hard drive's contents, including operating system, settings, applications and your own files) or you can back up just those files you have created – documents, photographs, music, etc. It is generally recommended that you do both because, while a system image contains everything, you can only use it for complete recovery in the event of situations such as hard drive failure. You cannot use it to restore individual files or groups of files that have become corrupted or been accidentally deleted. A system image should certainly be created when significant changes are made to the system or new applications installed, but given the frequency with which applications and operating systems are updated, many experts recommend that a system image is saved on a weekly basis. The files you have created yourself should be backed up at least this frequently and, if you are running a business, you will probably want to think about daily backup. Fortunately, backup is no longer the hassle it used to be. The facility to carry it out reliably and automatically is built into modern operating systems, and there are scores of third party applications, some of them free, that also aim to assist you with the task. Check up-to-date reviews to find the best products to meet your needs.

Where to back up

There are three basic choices:

- local storage on an external hard drive, DVD CD or flash drive;
- networked drives;
- online storage.

The options for all three are extensive. An external hard drive is generally best for full system backup, given the large amount of data that needs to be transferred. For regular backup of your own files, online storage is becoming ever more popular. The most important consideration is that you should not be backing up onto the same hard drive that contains your original files and, to guard against loss of data through theft or fire, the place where your backup data is stored should be separate from the computer on which it was created.

Passwords

Many of us are guilty of laxity as far as passwords are concerned. We choose words that we will remember easily, but which may be just as easily guessed by others. We use the same password in multiple situations, and we fail to change them when there is a chance that they might have become compromised.

A poorly selected password is almost as bad as no password at all. You should avoid drawing them from personal information, which can be easily guessed by people who have access to your details, and it is also wise to steer clear of standard dictionary words. The best passwords are those which mix numbers, upper and lower case letters and special characters in a manner that is unpredictable for anybody trying to access them. Of course, these are the most difficult passwords to remember, and you may wish to use mnemonics to help you remember them. Alternatively, you could purchase a password manager. These computer applications routinely generate high quality passwords, store them in an encrypted form, and may have an auto-insert facility to call them up when needed for online activity. Some password managers are better and more secure than others, so do check reviews before purchasing.

If you really have no alternative but to write passwords down, then at least keep them in a secure place and disguise the actual passwords in such a way that they will mean something to you but will be unintelligible to anybody else.

Physical security of equipment and data

These days we have access to so many reliable, cheap and versatile data storage devices that it's easy to lose track of the locations where information is held. With laptops, portable hard drives, data sticks and smartphones in abundance, you need to be organized if you are to stay in control. Whilst the effect of losing a data storage device might not be as dramatic for you as it has been in some of the cases that have hit the headlines in recent years, it is likely at the very least to cause some inconvenience, embarrassment and wastage of time. Here are a few measures you might consider to protect yourself:

1 When using multiple devices it's hard to keep track of the location that holds the latest version of a file you may be working on. You may find yourself losing the results of hours of work if you're not careful. The best way of ensuring this doesn't happen is to use one of the numerous cloud synchronization services such as Windows Live Mesh or Apple iCloud.

2 Limit the number of portable storage devices you use – you are asking for trouble if you carry multiple memory sticks around. Network or cloud services are generally a more reliable means of transferring data. If you're using such services for sensitive data, you may need to check that the level of encryption meets your requirements.

3 If you are using a portable device to transfer information between computers, make a habit of deleting the data it contains once the transfer is complete.

4 Destroy CD or DVD data discs as soon as they have fulfilled their purpose, and ensure that discarded hard drives are put beyond use.

5 Use specialist software to permanently and securely delete sensitive or confidential information that is no longer needed.

6 Protect laptops and phones with strong passwords. Portable devices are often configured to connect automatically to home or workplace networks. Leaving them insecure risks not only the data on the device itself but, in the event of loss or theft, may also leave the network wide open.

Protection from malicious attack

There are numerous packages available to protect your computer from internet-based attacks. Some quite competent applications even come free of charge. Read reviews in the computer press to find the most suitable applications to suit your needs. At the very least you should have a firewall in place, together with some anti-virus and anti-spyware software. Many of the commercial packages will also give you added security such as identity protection, password storage and e-mail security. But needless to say, you shouldn't just set up the protection and forget about it. New threats are constantly emerging, so it's important to initiate regular scans and updates.

Security of paper-based information

By now most people are aware that personal information contained in discarded documents may be used in the course of identity theft. It makes sense to have decent measures in place for the disposal of any paperwork containing your own details and, of course, you have a legal duty to deal appropriately with personal or sensitive information concerning others. Shredders are cheap enough and easy to use; it's really a matter of ensuring that you use them routinely. If you're buying a shredder for a home office setup, get the crosscut variety. They do a much better job of rendering a document unreadable than do the cheaper strip cut shredders.

SUMMARY

Effective storage of information requires:

- clarity about what is and is not worth filing;
- a simple and logical structure that is routinely adhered to;
- regular pruning of redundant material;
- attention to the security of your data.

USE TECHNOLOGY TO ASSIST

Technology may be both an aid to organization and a factor leading to greater disorganization. Technologically assisted generation and communication of information has led to a huge increase in the volume of information in daily circulation, and far from achieving the paperless office envisaged in the early 1980s, enormous quantities of paper are still being produced, handled and stored. Add to that the increasing use of e-mail and the biggest information repository of all, the internet, and you have a recipe for overload. But the tremendous capacity of technology to assist us in creating, communicating, manipulating and storing information also offers potential solutions to the problem. Your success in this will depend on judicious choice and effective use of the available tools.

KNOW WHEN NOT TO USE TECHNOLOGY

Information technology has become so all pervading that one may be tempted to use it for every information handling task.

This would be a mistake. There are occasions when the effort of using technology outweighs the advantage, or the medium is inappropriate:

- setting up a spreadsheet to produce a handful of one-off calculations that could be done quicker and just as reliably on a calculator;

- engaging in excessive internet research before embarking on a creative task, and finding yourself overwhelmed with other people's ideas before you have a chance to formulate your own;

- using e-mail, text messaging or instant messaging in unsuitable situations – for example, interactions requiring sensitivity or subtlety that call for face-to-face or, at the very least, telephone contact;

- using time and energy to learn a software package for a function that could be performed manually and has only marginal or occasional significance in your workload.

SOFTWARE CHOICES

Computer users and smartphone owners face a multiplicity of choice regarding the tools they might use on their devices. Alongside the established commercial office suites there are open source alternatives, often available free of charge, and options include applications that will reside on the individual's own computer, or may operate online in the cloud. One is frequently spoilt for choice when considering specialist software, and packages range hugely in terms of price and degree of sophistication. Then there are the myriad apps available to smartphone users. Estimates for the iPhone alone in 2012 put the number at some 500,000, with more appearing all the time. Often the choice of which tool to use will boil down to personal preference between similarly competent products.

The value of a particular package will vary from person to person. It will be dependent on how much you have used other similar products, your level of IT expertise, the way you like to work and the precise nature of your job. More sophisticated is by no means always superior. Often a simple application will meet a need better than one with all the bells and whistles. Many software providers make 30 day 'try before you buy' offers even on quite expensive products, enabling you to decide whether a package is right for your needs before committing funds to it. Use magazine reviews and recommendations to aid your decisions, but recognize that only you can make an accurate assessment of whether an application is worth having.

Let genuine needs drive your software decisions. It is all too easy to be enticed by the productivity claims of a particular software package, and having acquired it, to look around for a task on which to use it. Using a product to meet an identified need is generally an effective way of learning it, but take care not to set yourself unrealistic timescales for achieving your targets with a new application.

Before embarking on a new application, try to arrive at a realistic assessment of the benefits set against the investment of time in learning to use it. One way to do this is to estimate a payback period. The questions to ask yourself are:

- What will I use this package for?
- How much time per week do I currently spend doing these tasks?
- What are the weekly time savings I might reasonably expect once I'm a competent user of the package?
- How many learning hours will it take for me to achieve reasonable competence?

If you then divide the learning hours estimate by the figure for weekly time savings, you will arrive at an estimated payback period. For example, if it takes you ten hours to learn a package that only saves you 15 minutes a week, the payback period will be 40 weeks. In other words, it will be almost a year before you derive any time saving. In this situation, there are likely to be other time investments which will produce more immediate rewards.

Deciding to upgrade

Whatever software package or operating system you choose, there is likely to be an upgrade version available within a short time, promising new features and greater effectiveness. Make the decision whether to upgrade by seeking answers to the following questions:

1 Do I need the new features? Few of us use all the features of an application. New ones may sound attractive, but if they don't offer you significant benefits there is no point in acquiring them.

2 Are the advantages likely to be worth the cost and learning investment? Most upgraded packages will be broadly similar to their predecessors, but sometimes a major redesign will require a significant amount of relearning. Improvements may only be marginal, and it can be frustrating to discover that functions you have come to know and use regularly have vanished – spirited away into some unfamiliar menu or even removed entirely because developers have considered them less useful than the latest enhancements.

3 Will a hardware upgrade be required at the same time? A new package may put greater demands on your system, requiring increased memory or processor capacity. Check the minimum specifications before plunging in.

4 Does the package have a track record of reliability? These days software is so complex that despite extensive pre-release testing, it's quite common for there to be bugs and glitches in a new package that can prove very frustrating for the user. There may be incompatibilities that prevent other software from working or cause inexplicable crashes. Many experts recommend waiting until initial bugs have been ironed out before deciding to upgrade.

USEFUL TOOLS

We have already given some consideration in previous chapters to technology that may assist personal organization in specific areas of activity, but I'm going to give further attention here to applications that might provide organizational or time saving benefits to the average user. Clearly, in the available space I cannot do more than scratch the surface of what is available, and the examples given are but a snapshot of well-considered products at the time of writing. Books have a long shelf life, and any product I write about today may no longer be a leading contender in three or four years' time. In this respect computer applications are like racehorses. Favourites don't always stay ahead of the field, and from time to time unfancied runners come through to snatch the spoils.

Readers will wish to make their own investigations before acquiring any of the products mentioned or similar ones. In the following section I shall briefly consider the scope for better organization through the use of applications that aim to assist general office activity, aspects of time management, the organization of ideas and the management of notes. I'll also look at the various ways by which you might speed up the entry of data to your computer or smartphone.

General office activity

There can be few computer users who don't have at their disposal some form of general office suite – word processor, spread sheet and presentation software, etc – whether it's a standard desktop package such as Microsoft Office, an online freebie like Google Docs, or a cut-down package for smartphone. Unfortunately, applications such as word processors and spread sheets have become so ubiquitous that we may be guilty of almost taking them for granted. They are very powerful tools and most of us don't use them to anything like their full potential. We may tend to ignore some of the facilities that could save us time or enhance our personal organization.

Experienced users may also find that they are locked into ways of doing things that were learned when computers were slower and software less sophisticated, or that the trial and error way in which learning took place has bypassed important shortcuts. Half an hour revisiting the help file, manual or 'What's New?' summary for the software package may pay major dividends. Look for facilities you may have previously overlooked, or that weren't present in earlier versions. Check out operations that may simplify tasks, such as automatic formatting of documents, keyboard shortcuts on commonly used commands, or easy customization of toolbars, menus and templates to meet your particular needs.

Time management applications

To assist you in planning and tracking your time, there is a host of personal information managers available. Typically they will include a calendar, task lists which may be organized by category, context or project, contacts lists and e-mail management. Owners of both computer and smartphone will generally find the most useful products to be those that can readily synchronize data between different devices. For Windows machines the best-known and most widely used product is Microsoft Outlook. It doesn't have the strongest track record on usability and synchronization, although recent incarnations are a lot more user friendly than older versions. There are several well-regarded alternatives. Anyone seeking a free of charge application might like to take a look at Zimbra (www.zimbra.com) which is available as a download for Windows, Mac and Linux. It integrates e-mail, calendar, tasks and contacts into one easy to use package and has the ability to set rules for the management of e-mail, but is not as sophisticated as Outlook. Similarly, a combination of Google Calendar and

Google Mail will fulfil all the main PIM functions and is very easy to use, but lacks some of Outlook's integration. If you are happy to work with more than one product, each of which carries only some of the functions listed above then there are some excellent free packages and online services. Wunderlist (www.6wunderkinder.com) is highly rated for planning and managing task lists. It's free and available for all popular computer and smartphone operating systems. There are numerous other smartphone apps that fulfil aspects of the personal information manager role.

A second category of time management software includes those applications that issue timely reminders aimed at fostering better working habits. In Chapter 2 I mentioned RescueTime and ManicTime. These applications and others like them analyse your computer use and give you the ammunition to cut out the less productive elements of your day. Then there are various time prompting apps for both computer and phone. Daily Routine for the iPhone (www.dailyroutineapp.com) is directed at freelancers and homeworkers who have difficulty keeping to a set daily time-table. It allows you to schedule your day in detail with breaks included and issues gentle reminders when it is time for you to change your focus. Another iPhone app is Take a Break which reminds you with a vibration alert when it's time to get away from your computer and then shows you mobility exercises that can be performed unobtrusively during your break. There are a number of similar products for desktop computers. I have to say that I have found the ones I've sampled somewhat irritating after a while, but I think they may have a role in establishing better computer use habits.

A third group of time management applications includes those aimed at anyone who needs accurately to track time spent on tasks and associated expenses for the purpose of invoicing clients. These applications tend to be most useful on the phone rather than desktop computer. Two such iPhone products are Timewerks (www.sorth.com) and Time Master.

Organizing ideas

Getting your ideas into a shape where you can start to make sense of them and plan a way forward is often one of the most difficult elements of a new project, presentation or written assignment. For many of us it involves scribbled notes on jumbled scraps of paper that may not mean a great deal when we come to look at them again. Fortunately, there are a group of applications that can make the task easier.

Mind mapping software

Mind mapping software is helpful in the initial brainstorming phase of activity, allowing you to develop a visual scheme of the topics and subtopics that will comprise the activity, and to highlight the relationships between them (see Figure 8.1). Of course, you can do this on paper, but the value of using a computer application is that topics can be moved, merged and edited, relationships altered as your thoughts develop, without the need to redraw the whole map. The computer will do the donkey work,

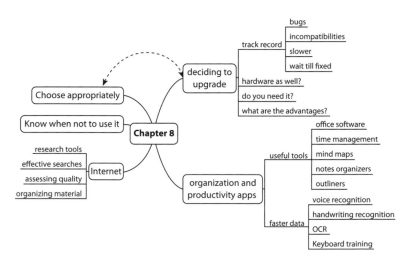

Figure 8.1 Mind map

leaving you to concentrate on your thoughts. There are numerous mind-mapping applications, both free and paid for. Two I like that have free versions are EDraw Mind Map (edrawsoft.com) and XMind (www.xmind.net)

Outliners

Outliners also work with topics and subtopics. They tend to be more structured than the free-form mind-map, and are often useful as a second stage after brainstorming. They allow you to progressively put more flesh on the bones of your document, building up its various levels, promoting, demoting or shifting topics, and collapsing or expanding elements so that you can alternately work upon detail and see the big picture. Some keep the text separate from content so that the outline structure is always visible.

There is a quite competent outliner included within Microsoft Word which often gets overlooked and, as ever, there are numerous other good examples, both freestanding and online, for desktop computers and mobile devices.

Notes organizers

You can use a notes organizer as a form of outliner, gathering together unformed snippets over time and then organizing them into a workable structure. But notes organizers have more going for them than just outlining, and warrant a section on their own. They are to my mind the most versatile of all tools for organizing thoughts and information from diverse sources in a flexible and accessible manner. Such applications provide you with a ready workspace where you can develop ideas, formulate objectives, build task lists and project outlines or pull together creative activity. They present you with a place to store and index the fruits of your research, including screenshots from websites, notes dropped in from other applications, and even elements of audio and video. They offer too a home for all those little bits of information that you want to keep but which don't fit with normal office applications, and which often end up on scraps of paper floating around your desk. There are any number of note organizing packages, but two of the most popular are EverNote and OneNote. Both are available on different operating systems and have the facility to synchronize between devices. With their access to online storage they are also great collaborative tools, allowing members of a team to work together on a document or project plan, with each member's contribution clearly identified.

The applications have different strengths and each has its fans. From the versions current at the time of writing (2012) I favour Microsoft OneNote, which comes with some versions of Microsoft Office, or can be purchased as a standalone item. It's nicely intuitive with an attractive notebook style that can be easily customized, and it integrates well with other applications in the Microsoft Office suite. For example, it's possible simply to designate an item in OneNote as a task entry in Outlook, with a target date and associated reminder if required. Once marked as completed in Outlook, the item will be updated in OneNote too. Similarly, mail messages in Outlook can be readily sent to OneNote. When saving web pages or screen clippings, you are able to choose the section where they will be filed in OneNote without leaving your browser or the programme with which you are working. Bright ideas have a habit of popping up when you are in the middle of something else and OneNote has a way of accommodating that without disrupting whatever else you are engaged upon. A simple keystroke combination brings up a side note on which you can record the idea and even link it to the document you are currently working upon.

RAPID INPUT OF DATA

The extent to which you can speedily and reliably input data to a computer, from where it may be manipulated, edited, distributed and stored, is clearly a factor in how well you are able to manage information. If you are a two finger typist, you may well despair of this aspect of your personal organization. Let's spend a few moments looking at four applications designed to help you.

Voice recognition software

With a voice recognition package you can dictate material via a microphone or digital voice recorder and the computer will convert your speech into text that can be directly fed into popular office programmes, e-mails and online posts. This type of software has been around for a number of years, but early packages conferred only limited benefits as they required the separate enunciation of each word in a manner that is difficult to achieve when speaking naturally. Increased processing power and ongoing software development mean that they now cope with normal speech, and producers claim up to 99 per cent accuracy with speeds of up to 160 words per minute – faster than even the most competent typist. But voice recognition is very complex technology seeking, as it does, to make sense of sounds delivered with a huge number of variables – diction, accent, modulation, emphasis – and users are still by no means unanimous in their acceptance of it.

When setting up a package you have to be prepared to spend some time training it to recognize your particular speech patterns and correcting a significant number of mistakes before the application becomes used to your voice. And you must continue a firm policy of correcting any errors in words or punctuation that crop up or, rather like an unruly pet, the software will repeat the misdemeanours and become less accurate.

You should remember too that dictation is a skill in itself. Many of us have difficulty articulating our thoughts cogently and fluently in a manner that will work well on paper. If you find yourself constantly having to backtrack and amend sections of text, it can remove some of the time savings. And because voice recognition software works partly by identifying words in context, it prefers speech that is delivered in fluent sentences. Unexpected pauses and any humming and hawing can play havoc with its accuracy.

For my part, I find that dictating directly into an application and correcting mistakes as I go along is not very conducive to fluency. When I do this, some of my attention is directed at the accuracy of what I have already said, rather than what I am about to say. I prefer to use a digital recorder and then to transcribe the resulting files, correcting any mistakes from the keyboard. It's important to do this within the application's own on-screen correction menu, as failure to do so will serve to perpetuate the errors.

Whilst I've been lukewarm about voice recognition in the past, I feel that the software and associated hardware have now developed to a point where I can happily use it as a reliable daily tool. I would particularly recommend it for those who have significant amounts of routine correspondence, or regularly need to transcribe rough notes to computer text. I'll confess that I haven't yet managed to achieve accuracy at the levels indicated by software producers, but for most routine text it delivers well into the 90 per cent bracket. This probably rivals my typing accuracy, but at speeds way in excess of those I can achieve from the keyboard. The leading voice recognition product on the market is Dragon Naturally-Speaking, distributed by Nuance (www.nuance.com). The company also offers Dragon Dictate for the Apple Mac and there are some voice recognition facilities in recent Windows and Mac operating systems. To make use of voice recognition, your computer will need a reasonably fast processor and plenty of memory. Check the minimum specifications carefully before buying.

Handwriting recognition

Through years of practice, we have become adept at jotting down key points while simultaneously carrying out another action – taking part in a meeting, holding a telephone conversation or exploring a difficult idea – and there are many instances where the ability to make a handwritten note and have it converted into editable computer text is extremely useful. Handwriting recognition has been around for a number of years, but early incarnations required users to learn quite complex scripting techniques and were often not very accurate. The advent of faster processors, greater memory capacity and increased portability of devices has brought forward a number of hardware items that are able to employ handwriting recognition and claim to make it easy and reliable – tablet computers and smartphones are the most prominent. For most purposes the keyboard is still quicker and more reliable than writing on a screen, but handwriting recognition has a role where use of the keyboard may be impractical – with smartphones for example where the virtual keyboard may be tiny, or in settings where use of the keyboard might be cumbersome, such as when taking notes in meetings or lectures. There are a number of apps for popular tablets and smartphones. Some claim increased accuracy with use as the software becomes accustomed to the user's script. Others aim to enhance the speed and accuracy of import by employing predictive capabilities.

Developments are ongoing and any reader thinking of acquiring a handwriting capable device or application should check up-to-date reviews. At the time of writing users and reviewers are still divided on the value of handwriting recognition applications, and the extent to which they work for you will depend, to a degree, on the quality and consistency of your script. If, like me, you have handwriting that even you have difficulty deciphering, then your computer may not have an easy time of it.

Optical character recognition (OCR)

I have already referred to OCR in relation to the scanning and filing of documents, but it deserves a further mention here as a technique for rapidly inputting data without the need for retyping. The latest OCR software will read a printed page and import it to a standard office application – word processor, spreadsheet or presentation package – with all formatting intact. For example, a table of figures can be scanned and dropped straight into Excel with cells accurately filled, and ready to be manipulated in whatever way you require. Pro versions of OCR packages such as OmniPage and ABBYY FineReader also include useful tools to transfer documents between different formats and turn paper forms into electronic ones.

Keyboard training packages

Keyboards aren't about to disappear wholesale from our computers. Even those who use the above methods of data input extensively will generally find themselves working with a keyboard some of the time. If you are a two-finger typist, you may benefit from the increase in typing speed that follows from developing the use of all your fingers. There are a number of inexpensive keyboard trainers available on CD or online that take you through staged development and practice. It is not unreasonable to look for a doubling of your speed with 8 to 12 hours of work. If you have been typing with two fingers for a long time, then you might find it a little more difficult to make the change, but as a former two-finger typist of 30 years' standing I can testify that the change is possible with a little perseverance and makes a considerable difference to productivity.

Activity – ask yourself

Take this opportunity to review your current software use, and ask yourself whether there are changes you could make that might assist your personal organization:

- What, if any, applications am I overusing or using inappropriately?

- With which applications that I currently use could I benefit from a review of my work habits in order to make better use of the available facilities and enhance my productivity?

- Are there applications that I do not currently use, but which I believe could make a significant difference to my productivity?

- Which of the above are likely to offer the best payback for the time I will spend learning new techniques or reviewing existing ones?

You might like to draw up a hit list in priority order – headed by those software-related tasks that offer the best payback – and incorporate it into your medium-term objectives and 'to do' list.

ORGANIZE INTERNET RESEARCH

The speed and ease with which you are able to access information on the world wide web can greatly assist with personal organization, but the sheer volume of information available presents several difficulties:

- separating the information you need from the mass of less relevant data;
- deciding when to stop searching;
- avoiding the distraction presented by other interesting but irrelevant material;
- assessing the quality and reliability of information.

The internet is huge and seductively accessible. You are just a couple of mouse clicks away from billions of pages of information, and the temptation is toward excessive searching, out of fear of missing some vital piece of information tucked away in the vast unruly collection. But resist the urge to seek information perfection. Nowhere does the 80:20 rule apply more than on the internet (80 per cent of the results come from 20 per cent of the effort) and you can waste large amounts of time chasing a rapidly diminishing addition to useful data. Concentrate, instead, on precise and well-planned searches that will get you quickly to manageable quantities of quality information.

Research tools

There are two primary vehicles for locating information on the Internet – directories and search engines. The vastly superior power and scope of search engines have made them pre-eminent, but directories are worth considering for some specialist research tasks.

Internet directories

Internet directories are compiled by human beings, and index sites under subject headings with progressively more specialist subheadings. Approaching an information gathering task via an Internet directory is rather like searching the catalogue of a library – fine for locating websites concerned with the subject you are interested in, but of limited value if what you're after is a specific reference that may be buried within a web page. You might want to use a directory if what you are looking for is a general overview within a topic area. Popular directories include the Open Directory Project (www.dmoz.org) and Yahoo Directory (http://dir.yahoo.com)

Search engines

Search engines are compiled and updated using web crawling software, which trawls the web looking for new pages and referencing the contents. This leads to much greater volumes of information than would be found in a directory and offers the ability to pull out references from deep within web pages. Locating the information you want is a matter of choosing the best combination of keywords. Google has the largest search engine database, and that makes it the engine of choice for a great many users. But not even Google contains anywhere near the sum total of searchable material on the net, so there is certainly value in using other search engines if you don't find what you are seeking on Google.

Meta search tools

These have no database of their own, but send the same enquiry to a variety of search engines, and may be useful if you're looking for a hard to find reference. One example is the quaintly named Dogpile (www.dogpile.com).

10 tips for effective searches

1 Formulate your search request with care. If you enter keywords that are too general, you risk being deluged with information. Search engines rank responses to queries with those that most nearly meet the search criteria at the top of the list, but a vague enquiry may throw up thousands of responses with similar rankings. Some lateral thinking may be necessary in choosing keywords likely to be in the material you are seeking.

2 Use inverted commas to enclose phrases when you wish the search engine to look for a complete phrase rather than the individual words that comprise it. This can sometimes get you more quickly to information you are seeking, especially when the words within the phrase are common ones.

3 Don't bother to include punctuation, capitals or small words such as prepositions in your search terms. Most search engines ignore them, so they won't benefit your results in any way.

4 Use the plus and minus symbols to narrow down your search. Preceding a search word with the minus symbol will exclude any results containing that word from the search, and can be handy for stripping out references unrelated to the information you are seeking. The plus symbol indicates that you specifically want a word included, and is useful when you wish to give a particular word priority or want the search engine to take account of small words that tend to be omitted from searches.

5 Filter by date. If you are searching for information that needs to be current, your task may be made more difficult by having to sort through older material. The 'more search tools' section

on Google allows you to confine your results to those sites which have been updated in the recent past.

6 If you are keen to keep abreast of the latest developments in an area of interest, perhaps to stay on top of your work or to keep tabs on the activities of competitor organizations, you might consider Google Alerts (www.google.com/alerts). This gives you access to e-mail notifications when websites that fulfil the search criteria are updated.

7 When presented with search results, don't just start by clicking on those items at the head of the list. Scan the first page or two of results in order to determine which are most likely to meet your requirements. However, don't waste time ploughing through multiple pages of results. If the information you are seeking isn't in the first 100 or so hits, it may be time to re-formulate your enquiry or use more sophisticated tools.

8 Get to know the search engine you use most frequently and take advantage of the advanced search section. Every search engine has one of these, offering sophisticated filters that may be extremely useful when you're experiencing difficulty unearthing what you require from a standard search.

9 Don't let yourself be distracted by links to other interesting but irrelevant pages. If something attracts your interest, use the bookmark facility to store a record of the location so that you can return to it at a later date.

10 A handy way of unearthing directories containing the resources you may be seeking is to include the word 'directory' within a search engine enquiry. For example, 'directory time management' will reveal directories that list time management courses and software.

Assessing quality

Finding information quickly is all very well, but what about the quality and reliability of what you discover? Within the billions of pages of information on the world wide web there is an awful lot of garbage. Anybody who wishes can quite simply set up a website and present information in an apparently authoritative way. So how do you discriminate between the reliable and the less so? Here are some pointers that may help:

- *Is the site the work of a reputable body?*
  Generally at the top of the list for reliability are: universities; national government information sites; local authorities; publicly funded bodies; known voluntary organizations; reputable companies; broadcasters; online versions of respected newspapers and periodicals.

- *Has the site been vetted in any way?*
  There are some sites and directories that make a positive commitment to verifying the quality of the links they carry. One such is About (www.about.com). Each of the categories in its directory is controlled by a specialist in the subject matter concerned.

- *Are there additional clues?*
  If a search comes up with information held on a website with which you are unfamiliar, you may get some clues regarding its reliability by considering the following:
  - Are references given for any facts and figures, research or survey results?
  - How up to date is the information? Does the web page show a 'last reviewed' date?
  - Does the information have a clear target audience and obvious purpose?
  - What is the presentation like? A slap-happy approach to spelling, grammar or presentation may indicate a similar attitude towards the veracity of information.
  - Are there any clues to the status and expertise of the originator?
  - Does the site contain links to other clearly reputable websites?

- *Am I able to double-check the information?*
  Similar information on different websites may offer some guide to validity, but take care. Identical or near-identical wording may indicate that it has simply been lifted from one site to the other.

- *Who uses the site?*
  To discover who is responsible for a site, how much traffic it receives, how many other sites link to it and what other sites the people who visit it use, go to www.alexa.com and type or paste the address (URL) of the site you wish to know about into the Search box.

Organizing the material you find

It's a simple enough matter to download pages for later reference or click on 'add to favourites' to save a link to an interesting or valuable site you may wish to visit again; but if you do a lot of internet research, you can quickly find your favourites list and the file location you use for downloads becoming cluttered and unwieldy. Use 'organize favorites' to set up appropriately labelled sub-folders within the favourites list and drop items from your list into the relevant folder. Similarly, create folders within your page download location that reflect either the subject matter of the downloaded pages or projects with which they are associated. Alternatively, you may wish to use a product such as PaperPort, Evernote or OneNote (all mentioned earlier) which have a useful facility for capturing screenshots of webpages as well as filing and indexing them. Be judicious in what you choose to save – links are generally more valuable than downloaded pages that may rapidly become out of date. It is also a good idea to schedule a regular pruning session to clear out any downloads or favourites that have become redundant.

SUMMARY

Modern information technology can be of considerable assistance in personal organization provided it is used appropriately. You need to:

- recognize the tasks for which technology offers no appreciable advantage;
- select software to meet identified needs;
- balance potential time savings against the commitment of time to learn new software applications;
- adopt precise search techniques when seeking information on the internet;
- monitor the quality of information obtained;
- manage and organize any saved material.

9

ORGANIZE YOURSELF AT HOME AND AWAY

In the first decade of the twenty-first century the British workforce grew by 4.8 per cent, but the number of self-employed home-workers increased by five times that amount. Almost two and a half million people now run businesses from their homes and many more are employed working wholly or partially from home or on the move. These figures are predicted to rise further as mobile technology and fast broadband continue to reduce the need for fixed work locations and rigid working hours. No book on personal organization would be complete without consideration of the special challenges presented by working from home or on the road.

WORKING FROM HOME

The range of working from home arrangements extends from those working full time in a self-employed capacity to those for whom an occasional bout of home working is an opportunity to escape the distractions of the office. But for everyone who spends a significant amount of time working from home, the organizational advantages and difficulties are fairly similar.

Advantages:

- control over your own schedule;
- nobody looking over your shoulder;
- freedom from some workplace distractions;
- flexibility to slot leisure or personal activity into what would normally be considered working hours.

Difficulties:

- absence of normal workplace structures;
- lack of supporting colleagues – may need to juggle different roles;
- potential new distractions;
- absence of boundaries between work and home life;
- workspace limitations.

Clearly you will wish to maximize the advantages and minimize the disadvantages, and all the points made earlier in the book about managing time and understanding the way you work will be of significance. But there are additional issues specific to home working in respect of balance, focus and workspace organization, which we might usefully look at now.

Balance

One of the biggest problems for home-based working is maintaining a balance between work and leisure. You are in control of your schedule, but unless you take care to set and maintain boundaries on your working day, you can find work beginning to invade all your waking hours and, without a degree of discipline, the work you do may not be very productive. With all the trappings of your home around you, there may be a tendency to flit between work tasks and leisure/family activity in a manner that reduces the effectiveness of your work and, because of guilt about neglected work tasks, does not permit full enjoyment of leisure activities.

To maintain a healthy and productive balance between work and leisure, build a structure to your working day. It may be helpful to see your day in terms of core time and flexible time using a broader approach to the common flexitime principle. The core time is that which will always be allocated to work or to family/leisure activity – no excuses, this time is sacrosanct. For example, you might decide that from 9 am until 2 pm every day is core working time and the period after 6.30 pm is core leisure time. The flexible time to make up your working week can move to accommodate a healthy leisure balance. One day might involve an early morning start, another some early evening work and a third might follow traditional office hours. Provided you have a significant block of working time that becomes routine and that your family, friends and clients are able to tune into, you can take advantage of the flexibility that working from home offers to improve your lifestyle.

Balance also features in the way you structure your working hours to ensure you get the best out of yourself and give adequate attention to the different aspects of your work. You need to focus not only on those core activities that bring in the money, but on the maintenance tasks too: those routine jobs that keep you functioning properly – staying informed, dealing with correspondence and organizing your workspace.

Before 09.00	09.00 – 14:00	14:00 – 18:30	After 18:30
Flexible Time	Core Work Time	Flexible Time	Core Leisure Time

Figure 9.1 Flexible working day

In a traditional work setting, there are likely to be others whose specialist roles support your own. Chances are that when you are working from home it's all down to you. As well as fulfilling your main role, you may find that you are acting as your own office manager, PA, bookkeeper, marketing executive and odd job person. It may be impracticable or uneconomic to employ others in these capacities, and so you need to find ways by which the full range of activity required for success will be achieved. Rather than allowing tasks to build up until you are forced to have a bookkeeping splurge or a filing blitz, generate a varied work schedule to instil painless habits by weaving the different roles into your daily or weekly routine. Ask yourself the following questions:

- What are the various roles I need to fulfil? (List them.)
- Roughly what proportion of my time will be taken up by each of these?
- How does the market rate for these roles compare with the price per hour that I would put on my time in my main role?

When you are clear about the answers, you might like to consider a formal working arrangement to ensure the necessary services are fulfilled. If, for example, you decide that two hours a week is necessary for bookkeeping you might regard yourself as under contract to provide that service for one hour every Tuesday and Thursday, and approach the duty in just the same frame of mind as if you had been externally hired to fulfil the role. Similarly, you might act as a general administrator for half an hour every day. Visualizing your different roles in this way can help you get to grips with them all and prevent some from being undervalued or overlooked. Putting a price on the various roles also helps you get a handle on those tasks that it might make sense to contract out.

Focus

Who reminds you about things that need to be done? Who keeps your motivation high and helps out when you hit a tricky work problem? It's probably all down to you once again. But time and workload organization can help make up for the absence of colleagues and mentors:

- It's even more important when you are working on your own to plan your activities over different time frames, to set clear, manageable challenges and to break down long-term projects into smaller chunks. It makes tasks easier to handle and gives you that much needed sense of progress.

- Stay on top of your schedule by whatever means suits you – paper-based or electronic – but stick to one simple system.

- Consider using checklists of daily and weekly routine tasks so that nothing gets missed.

- Break up your week with activities that involve human contact, and take steps to build and maintain your networks. Isolation is a frequent problem for those working from home. Other people similarly engaged can provide much needed advice and support.

Appropriate workspace

Attention to good organization of your workspace can give a significant boost to productivity. The idea of firing off e-mails from the comfort of your bed or mapping out your business plan on a sun-drenched patio may be attractive and, indeed, there may be tasks that you can fulfil comfortably and effectively in unconventional settings, but the likelihood is that for a significant portion of your work, some form of office space is a must. Your home office does not have to be grand – forget those extravagant Sunday supplement conversions – but it should be comfortable and functional with attention paid to a layout that suits your working needs. Too often we neglect, in our home working arrangements, features that we would regard as essential if we were working elsewhere. We give ourselves insufficient or inappropriate space, and use the furniture and equipment that is to hand rather than spending a small amount of time and money creating a working environment that meets our requirements. Take account of the recommendations in Chapter 6 and consider the following fundamental elements:

- **A door you can close when necessary.**
  Working on the dining room table may be convenient, but it presents a packing-up task every time you finish work for the day, and may also render you more open to interruption if other household members are present. Perhaps most importantly, it increases the difficulty of separating working life and home life.

- **A well-proportioned and adjustable chair.**
  Often neglected, this is probably the most important investment you will make.

- **A work surface that is sufficiently spacious to accommodate essential equipment and gives you plenty of free space.**
  It doesn't have to be a fancy desk; there are plenty of inexpensive, well-designed models available, and even foldaway options that could be considered if you are working in a multi-function area.

- **A pleasant, well-lit and comfortable environment.**
  Working in a dingy boxroom, surrounded by piles of junk, has an effect on your work after a while.

- **Adequate storage equipment.**
  If space is at a premium, go upwards rather than outwards. Shelves and stackable boxes may make up for a shortage of floor space.

There will be other factors to consider, depending on the nature of your work. If it involves clients visiting you, what sort of space do you have to receive them, and are there any local business restrictions or covenants that could lead to difficulty? If a great deal of your work is done on the telephone, do callers always receive a professional response, and might it be worth installing a second line with separate voicemail facilities? A second line can also be a valuable way of ensuring that work and leisure do not overlap. Set the work line to receive voicemail during your leisure time and do the same with the home line during your working hours.

There are other issues – legal, fiscal, regulatory – that may come into play with home working arrangements, particularly if your activities involve the employment of others, premises modification or the setting up of a space to be wholly and exclusively used as an office. But such matters are beyond the scope of this book. There are numerous other books and internet sites offering useful information and advice. Whatever the nature of your home-based work, take the trouble to clarify your needs, research any areas of uncertainty and organize yourself accordingly.

ORGANIZING YOURSELF AWAY FROM THE OFFICE

If your work takes you regularly out on the road, you will be familiar with the organizational challenges such activity presents. For you it is a matter of keeping on top of your schedule, maintaining effective communication with your base, and ensuring that information you need is to hand and that equipment does not let you down. You share some of the challenges of balance and focus that are faced by those working from home. However, this section is directed not so much at those who are regularly on the road and are accustomed to the demands of mobile working as at the rest of us, for whom a trip away from the office is a more occasional event and one that may signal major disruption.

Business trips and conferences can put a large spanner in your personal organization works. In the hours prior to your departure, you find yourself scurrying around to complete tasks that won't wait until your return. You finally manage to get away, drained and ratty, only to discover when you get to your destination that you have left a vital document behind. In the course of your trip you are pestered by messages relating to a minor crisis, resolution of which is dependent on a piece of information that lurks somewhere in your filing system. Finally, you arrive back, exhausted, burdened with new work and facing a backlog of correspondence, voicemail and e-mail messages.

The key to retaining your equilibrium, when work takes you away from the office for days at a time, is good planning and adherence, wherever possible, to normal routines.

Planning

- **Build some space into your schedule.**
  Scale back on any non-urgent work in the couple of days prior to your departure so that you can concentrate on those tasks that have to be completed before your return. Always allow more time for this than you think you will need.

- **Cover your home base.**
  Ensure that you have somebody who can check your mail, handle any minor crises, and find their way around your filing system and the information on your computer. Make sure you leave accurate contact numbers.

- **Check and double-check that you have everything you need for the trip.**
  Don't be tempted to take lots of additional work in the vain hope that you will find time to deal with it. You are bound to come back with more than you took.

- **Put together an 'out of office kit'.**
  This should comprise day-to-day accessories – envelopes, mini-stapler, pens, batteries. Keep this handy so you can just drop it into your briefcase when you have a trip to make.

- **If you have a number of locations to visit, plan the order to minimize travelling time.**
  Journey-planning software may be of assistance in this.

- **Make sure that you know how to carry out any unfamiliar tasks.**
  These include picking up your voicemail messages remotely, accessing e-mail via the web or tapping into your organization's network while on the road. Don't just trust to instructions from somebody else. Check the operation for yourself before you leave, to ensure it works. There is nothing worse than assuming that you will be able to stay in touch and then finding that you can't.

- **Most importantly, make sure that you have any passwords you need to access the above-mentioned facilities.**

- **Change your voicemail message and set up e-mail auto-response so that callers know you are away and when you will be back.**
  Include a mobile number if appropriate. Remember to change these messages when you return.

- **Check that you have everything you need installed on your laptop computer or phone.**
  Synchronize your data and ensure you have all relevant software, reference and contact material. The capacity and connectivity of today's portable devices means that you should be able to accommodate the same level of information as exists on your desktop machine.

- If you are using public transport, earmark some tasks that are particularly appropriate for completion while travelling.
  Normally this will mean tasks that are not reliant on major paper shuffling, and can put up with some degree of interruption.

- Don't underestimate the debilitating effect of travel.
  Allow some breathing space in your schedule before pitching into meetings and appointments.

- If your trip involves foreign travel, check that you have all the adapters and rechargers you need to keep your equipment on the go.
  Make sure also that your mobile phone is set up to receive calls in the country or countries you are visiting.

- If your laptop is set automatically to download updates to its operating system, security software or applications, you may want temporarily to disable this facility.
  It can be very frustrating, and potentially quite expensive, to find yourself in the middle of a lengthy download when you simply wish to check your e-mails during a brief stop at an airport or internet hotspot.

Maintaining routines

- Resist the temptation to bundle up conference papers, 'to be sorted out when I get back'.
  They will be destined to remain a disorganized bundle. Deal with any paperwork you receive while on the road in the same way as you would in the office (use the five Ds) and be particularly energetic with the 'discard' category.

- Try to set some time aside during your day for dealing with routine correspondence and messages.
  When you tap into your e-mail and voicemail, deal with as much of it as possible, rather than just scanning through for major problem messages. This way, you will greatly ease the backlog of work waiting for you on your return.

- Set up a working area in your hotel room that is as conducive to productivity as possible.
- Keep track of expenses as you go.
  It's much easier than trying to remember them afterwards.
- Give yourself a break.
  On conferences and business trips you can find yourself talking shop from breakfast until late evening. Build in some rest and relaxation if you don't want to return frazzled and exhausted.
- Plan your first day back in the office before you return, but don't try to fit in too much.

SUMMARY

When working from home, you should ensure:

- a balance between work and leisure;
- a balanced approach to the varied roles you may need to fulfil;
- attention to maintaining focus;
- good work space organization.

Operating away from your normal base requires effective planning to counteract the absence of facilities you normally take for granted, and maintenance of good work routines.

KEEP UP THE GOOD WORK

We are all familiar with the phenomenon of resolution fatigue. Good intentions launched with enthusiasm and vigour on 31 December are abandoned and forgotten by 10 January. It's no different with decisions to improve personal organization. Reading this book is a start, but it won't bring all the results you want without some effort on your part.

REVIEW YOUR OBJECTIVES

In Chapter 1 I invited you to set some objectives in respect of better personal organization. No doubt you will have made progress with these as you have worked your way through the book, and hopefully too you will have gained new ideas on how you might tackle the organizational weaknesses you identified at the outset. It's now time to take stock. I would like to suggest that you review and refine your objectives, adjusting your priorities where necessary and setting target dates as required. Go back to the list you drew up in Chapter 1 and ask yourself the following three questions:

1 Which of these items, if any, have already been fully achieved? (Cross them off.)

2 What amendments do I wish to make to the remainder as a result of reading this book?

3 Are there areas of concern that I did not originally identify, but that I now realize require my attention?

Look at your amended list and prioritize the items on it A or B according to your estimate of their value in lifting your current level of personal organization. The priority A items are the most important, the ones to concentrate on first. Set yourself an action plan for them, breaking down each major objective into its constituent tasks together with target dates. If you're carrying out this exercise on paper, you may wish to use a simple table format such as the one shown in Figure 10.1 to assist in drafting your proposals. When you're happy with your action plan, enter tasks and dates into whatever time-tracking system you are using, and get cracking with implementation. Don't take on too much at once. Remember that you need to give new habits time to become established.

CHECK YOUR PROGRESS

Review progress regularly, weekly if possible, but not less than monthly. Give yourself immediate positive reinforcement or reward for every step forward, and use your successes as stepping stones to further achievement. Be kind with yourself when you have failed to achieve the progress you anticipated. Look for the reasons: perhaps you were trying to achieve too many things at once, maybe you didn't bash away for long enough to establish a new habit. Don't let yourself be lured into abandoning your goals, however. Reframe them and move on.

Action plan

Main objective:

Target date:

Sub-goals and tasks	Start date	Target date

Figure 10.1   Action plan

Visualize the way that you will work and the benefits that will accrue when you have perfected the new skills and ways of working. Visualization is a very powerful means of seeing you through the short-term pain and into the long-term gain. Once your priority A objectives are well under way, you can move on to priority B.

FIND WAYS OF STAYING ON TRACK

Be on the lookout for any means by which you can keep your objectives at the front of your consciousness and your motivation high. For example, you might find it useful to adopt a weekly points system that rewards or penalizes you for aspects of good or bad organization. Points might be awarded along the following lines:

- +10 points for every day planned in advance;
- −10 points for every 'to do' item carried over for more than one day;

- –10 points for every task performed that could have been delegated;

- +10 points for an empty filing tray at the end of the week;

- –2 points for every item in your filing tray in excess of 20 at the end of the week;

- –2 points for every e-mail message not dealt with on the day it is received;

- –2 points for each additional day that an e-mail message continues not to be actioned.

Your aim, of course, is to finish each week in credit. Don't simply adopt the suggestions above, but choose your points allocation and the areas on which you will concentrate to suit your own situation. Give yourself a level of challenge that is achievable and don't try to take on too many things at once. As your organization improves, so you can make things tougher for yourself.

WHAT IF OLD HABITS REAPPEAR?

You will be very fortunate if you don't experience setbacks in the process of building new, more organized habits. Your old habits are likely to have been acquired over many years, and you can't expect to shift them at the drop of a hat. But setbacks shouldn't be a signal to engage in despair, self-condemnation and abandonment of hard-won gains. We're all a mixture of strengths and weaknesses, and self-development seldom progresses in a straight line. Relapses can even be viewed as opportunities to review, reflect, regroup and plan the next stage of development, armed with knowledge of where the difficulties lie.

Here's what do when old habits start to reappear:

- Reflect on what you have been able to achieve, secure in the knowledge that what you've done once, you can do again.

- Rather than succumbing to guilt about your failure to be organized, visualize the positives. Reinforce in your mind once more the control over your life that achieving your objectives will bring, and recapture your feelings of enthusiasm at the prospect of being organized.

- Examine the reasons why the setbacks have occurred. Have they arisen as a result of additional burdens, increased stress, out of the ordinary events, or simple loss of focus? Some of the pressures may have been unavoidable, whereas it may be possible to address others so that they don't cause you problems in future.

- Finally, having taken stock and rekindled your motivation, revisit the strategies suggested in this book, set new targets and work to get yourself back on track.

You can do it!

Creating Success series

Dealing with Difficult People by Roy Lilley
Decision Making & Problem Solving by John Adair
Develop Your Assertiveness by Sue Bishop
Develop Your Leadership Skills by John Adair
Develop Your Presentation Skills by Theo Theobald
Effective NLP Skills by Richard Youell and Christina Youell
How to Deal with Stress by Stephen Palmer and Cary Cooper
How to Manage People by Michael Armstrong
How to Organize Yourself by John Caunt
How to Write a Business Plan by Brian Finch
How to Write a Marketing Plan by John Westwood
How to Write Reports & Proposals by Patrick Forsyth
Improve Your Communication Skills by Alan Barker
Successful Project Management by Trevor Young
Successful Time Management by Patrick Forsyth
Taking Minutes of Meetings by Joanna Gutmann

The above titles are available from all good bookshops.
For further information on these and other Kogan Page titles,
or to order online, visit the Kogan Page website at
www.koganpage.com